WHAT

## THE KNIGHT'S CODE ...

"*The Knight's Code* is a major piece of the puzzle in this new season that God is creating in men's ministry today. It isn't a theory, but a handbook in guiding men on how to become the warriors they were created to be. If you are a man that believes Jesus is only meek, gentle, and safe, then don't read this book, as it isn't for you, but if you are a man that desires change, get some guys together, walk through this, and watch God recreate passive Christian men into unstoppable, undefeatable 'knights' for the King of Kings."

—BRAD STINE, comedian, communicator, and author
who *New Yorker* Magazine called "God's Comic"

"Over the past thirty-five years of counseling, coaching, and mentoring men, I have seen a common problem—confusion concerning what identity in Christ is supposed to look like and how to live it out day by day. Too hard and macho? Too soft and weak? We know intuitively and instinctively that we will not have the satisfaction we seek as men until we find the proper balance.

Much of this confusion comes as a result of how Jesus has been represented to us. In an attempt to communicate a compassionate Christ, many preachers, authors, artists, and filmmakers have instead created a picture that portrays Jesus as weak and effeminate. To be His follower would mean I am to look like that as well. Yes, Jesus had the gentle side that unashamedly loved people. But He was also a man's man that could run the moneychangers out of the temple with a whip, stand up to the religious abusers of his day, and, ultimately, endure the brutality of the scourging and crucifixion.

What Robert Noland has done with *The Knight's Code* is help men have both a clear vision and workable plan of how to be the kind of **MAN** they were created to be—strong, courageous, compassionate, and relentless in pursuit of Kingdom purposes. I highly recommend this book to every man who truly desires to move from ordinary to extraordinary!

—DR. ED LAYMANCE, PhD, LPC, LMFT

*Special Thanks*

*Jesus—the only King worthy to follow.*

*Robin, Rhett, and Rheed—the best wife and sons
I could possibly ask for or imagine.*

*The men who have walked with me on this
journey and allowed me to share their stories.*

*Jason & Amy—for transforming text to art.*

## Recommended Applications for The Knight's Code

- Read for yourself to challenge and inspire your walk with God.

- Read, discuss, and process in a group of peers.

- Read and lead to disciple a younger group of men.

- Read and lead with your teenage son(s) to deal with key men's issues.

- Any men's group, Sunday school, or discipleship setting.

Discussion questions are at the end of each chapter with an overview wrap-up session at the end of the book.

# THE KNIGHT'S CODE

LIVE PURE
SPEAK TRUE
RIGHT WRONG
FOLLOW THE KING

## ROBERT NOLAND

*The Knight's Code*
Published by 517 Resources, Inc.
Burleson, TX 76028


Copyright © 2010 Robert Noland
517 Resources, Inc.
First Edition Printed in the U.S.A 2010


Cover Design: Jason Bradley
Interior Design: Amy Balamut
Author Photo: Rheed Noland


ISBN 978-0-9829130-0-0

www.theknightscode.com

# CONTENTS

THE KNIGHT'S CODE

FOR MORE
INFORMATION
AND
RESOURCES,

VISIT
WWW.THEKNIGHTSCODE.COM

## CHAPTER 1

# WHY SHOULD YOU READ THIS?

*"I need something more! For if I know the law but still can't keep it, and if the power of sin within me keeps sabotaging my best intentions, I obviously need help! I realize that I don't have what it takes. I can will it, but I can't do it. I decide to do good, but I don't really do it; I decide not to do bad, but then I do it anyway. My decisions, such as they are, don't result in actions. Something has gone wrong deep within me and gets the better of me every time." —Paul in Romans 7:18–20* MSG

Why should you read this? That's a fair question and I want to answer it. Because if you're going to commit a few hours of your life to this book—or longer, if you're going through it with a group—you deserve to understand the real premise, the heart of this project.

If you're like me at all, you often start the first chapter of this type of book believing that the author is some kind of expert and maybe this will be the one that's going to change your life.

Please allow me to interject a personal disclaimer right now. I did not write this book because I am an expert on anything, or have it all together, or have anything mastered, so now I can impart to you all that wisdom. I am not making that claim. But I am now into my 50th year of life and 30th year of ministry. In that time, I have experienced and witnessed a great deal about men on this journey.

So my purpose in this book is two-fold. First, I have had to face the consistent issues and problems in my own life, as well as address them in the lives of the men that I have discipled. The same issues and problems that Paul was referring to in the opening passage. His gut-level honest confession shows his frustration with what he does versus what he doesn't do, what he doesn't do versus what he actually does. We're talking the Apostle Paul here, gentlemen! The guy who was personally confronted by Jesus while on a murderous rampage against Christians, yet the guy who eventually wrote the bulk of the New Testament. His letters and my intent lead to the same place and my second purpose for this book: to declare that Jesus Christ alone is the prescription for our ills as men and the solution to the issues that create our pain.

In all my years of ministry, I have taken on a lot of different roles inside and outside the church, and in doing so, a consistent calling for me has been to men and connecting them with Jesus. I have sat with many guys weeping over their sin. I have sat with men weeping over all that they just realized they lost. I have also sat with many men who would arrogantly proclaim they were doing great without God. I have witnessed addictions of every kind and a whole laundry list of things that humans can run to, instead of God, as I myself have done all too often. I have also had the privilege of celebrating with brothers who overcame great personal obstacles.

Each situation, including my own, has proven that the real difference between healing or Hell, deliverance or decadence, is not how you solve the problem, but rather, what you do with Jesus *in* the problem. Allowing Him to reach into the recesses of our wretchedness and redeem every last drop of our humanity. And that, my friend, is a life-long commitment and process.

Inside these pages, we will delve into the dark issues of manhood, but please know we will always unapologetically point to Christ as our only Source of healing, our only Hope of deliverance. If you are not sure about this "Jesus stuff," I want to challenge you to open your mind and keep reading. At the end of the book, the worst case scenario is you wasted some time. But what if you find some real answers?

## ARE WE THERE YET?

Over the years, I have heard the buzz begin about a new men's book. I've heard guys discussing concepts and one-liners. They are enthralled by the author's grasp of the issues. But—and this is a big but—I have just as often watched those same guys go back to the same issues they had before reading the book. Life on the "back cover side" of the book looked no different than life on the "front cover side" of the book. Now, is that the author's fault? Maybe not. But basically, the experience equals watching a good movie. I enjoyed it, I was entertained, but it didn't change anything. Did you get your money's worth? If the goal was Christian entertainment, yeah, you did.

> WHY DOES LIFE ON THE "BACK COVER SIDE" OF THE BOOK OFTEN LOOK NO DIFFERENT THAN LIFE ON THE "FRONT COVER SIDE" OF THE BOOK?

*"So, Robert, what's your point?"* This book is not—repeat, not—written to be entertainment, not a conceptual, theoretical read, but a practical, application-oriented, change-your-life handbook. If you aren't really interested in change or you just want to inhale another Christian men's book to say you read it, put the book down, and find a better book. Yep, there are way better books out there for that than this one, so don't waste your time here. ... BUT if you're ready to do something about the direction of your life, marriage, fatherhood, purity, integrity, and so on, then read and apply the action points. Apply, apply, apply. The reading's not the key. It's the application. Simply reading this book will do you zero good, but applying what you read will. That's why going through this book with a group of guys will likely be more effective than alone.

If everyone who read the Bible truly applied God's principles, we'd be living in a vastly different world right now. So, this life change thing requires Biblical truth leading to principles of application, driven by a man's desire to obey.

*Do not merely listen to the word, and so deceive yourselves. Do what it says. Anyone who listens to the word but does not do what it says is like a man who looks at his face in a mirror and, after looking at himself, goes away and immediately forgets what he looks like. But the man who looks intently into the perfect law that gives freedom, and continues to do this, not forgetting what he has heard, but doing it—he will be blessed in what he does. —James 1:22–25* NIV

Let's go down that road with James for a minute. All religions or belief systems assume you are ignorant of their ways when you first believe or begin to learn their doctrine. You are then taught through their "truth," or the "ways of the force," so to speak. When you understand those points, you become enlightened or move into revelation or knowledge. Most of the world's ways teach that if you go from ignorance (not knowing) to knowledge (knowing), you have thus arrived. You get what they're teaching. For those belief systems, "understanding" is arriving. Well, just because I "understand" where Hawaii is and "understand" what all the islands offer does not mean I have "arrived" and am experiencing Hawaii. There's only one way to do that—go there.

Here's another example and I'll be personal. I went to college and graduated with a business degree with a minor in communication. I ended up with a very expensive piece of paper that said I had gone from ignorance to knowledge in the area of business and communication. Our American culture, the corporate world, and of course, my proud wife and mom agreed I had what was needed to do good business and talk coherently in front of people. I can tell you in all humility that upon graduation, I had not a clue of how to do either. Sure, I had a grasp on a lot of great concepts that I believed to be true. But I lacked one very important element that would eventually make all the difference in the world in my two areas of "expertise": real world experience.

Now, to be clear, I am a big "get your education" advocate. A college degree is a great asset. But think about your own journey. How

did you get good at what you do? And how many of us end up doing something vastly different than our education states we should be
good at? My point is when everyone says we have arrived at knowledge is rarely when we have arrived at all!

In a discussion on parenting, which couple often appears to know
the most about that subject? The newlyweds with no kids or a couple
married six years with a four year old and a two year old? Usually in my
experience, after talking to the newlyweds with no kids, they would
be the clear winners. Why? Because the knowledge of all they plan to
apply one day sounds amazing. The stuff they have read on-line about
parenting can make them sound like Mr. Rogers and Mother Teresa
having babies! But go interview the couple with the two kids around
bath and bedtime? What you will hear, through the mother's desperate sobbing after an impossible day, is the real world. The knowledge
can sound great, but how did it actually work out in real life? If you're
a parent, you know that nine times out of ten, you go with your gut,
not your head. That gut is developed through commitment coupled
with experience. The same is true for us as Christian men. We grow
by commitment coupled with experience. And there's only one way to
gain experience. Go there.

## OUR GOD IS A 'HANDS ON' GOD

Jesus changed everything upon His arrival, including what a true
belief or faith should require. He wanted His disciples to not just understand, but to apply. Life to God is hands on. Not a classroom lec-
ture hall with a chalkboard, but a technical school full of tools. When
we follow Jesus, "arrival" is application, not simply understanding. The
disciples didn't arrive until they had lived it out with Him. He didn't
teach them and then go off and leave them. He doesn't do that with
you and me either. In simple terms, this relationship isn't like Yoda
and Luke Skywalker, but more Rocky Balboa and Mick the trainer. He
doesn't release you into the Dark Side alone with the occasional mind

control moment. He stays in your corner to coach you, cheer you on, kick your butt, dress your wounds, and smile when you win a round. Even when He ascended to Heaven, He promised He would always be present—just in a new way (Matthew 28:20).

Think about it. Where in the Bible do you see Jesus teaching and don't find Him immediately before or after being involved in doing ministry? He was constantly showing them (us) what to do. He was constantly inviting His disciples into what He was doing. "Oh, you want to walk on the water? Okay, step out of the boat." "Oh, you want to feed thousands of people, but have no food? Go get me that little boy's lunch, got something I want to show you." Jesus was fueling, training, and preparing His followers for life after the Cross.

## BELIEVE & BECOME

The Church you attend today is a result of those early Christians applying their knowledge, not simply believing in something or someone. What if Peter had just decided he had been enlightened and that was enough? No, he believed it, so he became it. He changed into what he believed. When you trace Peter from the denial of Christ to the preaching at Pentecost, anyone would have to admit, something major happened to this guy! He had become!

> YOU ARE TO BELIEVE, SO YOU CAN BECOME.

I want to repeat this point and make it personal.

We are to believe, so we can become.

You are to believe, so you can become.

The goal is becoming. How? By practice through obedience. Expressing faith.

Since I dissed Yoda earlier, let me quote him here: "Do or do not. There is no try."[1]

You think Peter would have been crucified upside down for just believing something? Don't think so. Peter was nailed upside down for his what … ? Yeah, his actions! He just couldn't seem to stop practicing this Jesus thing, so they had to kill him too to shut him up. Check this out …

*"And what more shall I say? I do not have time to tell about Gideon, Barak, Samson, Jephthah, David, Samuel and the prophets, who through faith conquered kingdoms, administered justice, and gained what was promised; who shut the mouths of lions, quenched the fury of the flames, and escaped the edge of the sword; whose weakness was turned to strength; and who became powerful in battle and routed foreign armies. Women received back their dead, raised to life again. Others were tortured and refused to be released, so that they might gain a better resurrection. Some faced jeers and flogging, while still others were chained and put in prison. They were stoned; they were sawed in two; they were put to death by the sword. They went about in sheepskins and goatskins, destitute, persecuted and mistreated—the world was not worthy of them. They wandered in deserts and mountains, and in caves and holes in the ground. These were all commended for their faith, yet none of them received what had been promised. God had planned something better for us so that only together with us would they be made perfect." —Hebrews 11:32–40 NIV*

Note the many thousands of nameless believers that sacrificed and made sure we even have a faith to live out!

Jesus didn't say, "Please, kids, don't try this at home. I am a trained God-Man." He taught us to practice these things—at home, at your work, with your friends, as you go through life.

*Therefore everyone who puts these words of mine into practice is like a wise man who built his house on the rock. The rain came down, the streams arose, and the winds blew and beat against that house; yet it did not fall because it had its foundation on the rock. —Matthew 7:24–25 NIV*

If you "put something into practice," you take the concept from belief to action. A doctor in practice is administering care to patients. A lawyer in practice is administering expertise to clients. A Christian in practice is administering Jesus to the world.

Let's say you get sick and just can't shake it. You call a doctor and go to his office. He walks in and you tell him all your symptoms. He responds, "Well, I believe you are sick, sir. And I believe all I learned in medical school and the current journals and studies I am reading could help you. However, I'm just not ready to make the commitment of diagnosing what's wrong with you and offer solutions."

You're desperate and with your fever so high, you're not even sure you didn't hallucinate what you just heard, so you whimper, "Doc, can you just write me a prescription?" He shakes his head, "No. I believe I can help you, but that would take far too much commitment on my part. I would be practicing at that point and I just can't do that." … Ridiculous scenario? Yeah. But aren't we often guilty of this very thing with our own faith in the lives of the people around us who need help?!

*Jesus, undeterred, went right ahead and gave his charge: "God authorized and commanded me to commission you: Go out and train everyone you meet, far and near, in this way of life, marking them by baptism in the threefold name: Father, Son, and Holy Spirit. Then instruct them in the practice of all I have commanded you. I'll be with you as you do this, day after day after day, right up to the end of the age." —Matthew 28:18–20 MSG*

Who is the "you" in that last promise statement? It was them! It is us! You. Me. All His followers. Jesus was communicating a lifestyle, which the disciples carried on and lived out, just as He asked and prayed for. So, how are we doing?

## BELIEF VS. ACTION

Let's give a basic, simple, safe modern-day example. Even the casual church attender knows the Bible teaches about tithing. A tithe is 10 percent. Most Christians believe that at least a tithe should be given to the Church. In fact, the only place in Scripture where God tells us to test Him is found in Malachi 3 and it has to do with tithing and giving. If you go up to most men on a Sunday morning that are sitting in a pew and ask them what they believe the Bible teaches about giving to the church, what will most of them say? Yep, a Christian should tithe. That means at least 10 percent of the income is given. Now … how many of those same men actually tithe? Open up the W-2 in January and then get the annual church giving statement out and do the math. It's real easy. For the average income, you made about $65,500 last year? The church statement should be $6,550. Is it? How far off was it? How much did you believe it?

See the difference? Saying we believe we should do something versus actually doing it. As Paul said, "I decide to do good, but I don't really do it." Knowing versus practicing. That's how we tell what we really believe. Actions. How does your wife know you love her? She just believes she is loved? She just knows it? How far did that one get you on the last anniversary or Valentine's Day? Reality is you have to practice attention, listening, compliments, hugs, kisses, creating security, right? Most marriages don't end because the husband just wouldn't believe what he should do. They end because he didn't practice the right things. We believe a lot of concepts in Christianity that we don't actually apply, we don't actually do. So, that begs the question in light of the New Testament: Do we really believe that which we *don't* do? Do we really believe that which we *won't* do? (My humble answer is no. And this is all true for me as well.)

## STAY OPEN & PRAY FOR TRUTH

There is a strong chance that you are reading this book because you are a Christian man and your goal is life change. But maybe you aren't a believer in Jesus Christ, but were intrigued by the Knight's theme and you are looking for answers in becoming a man of character. Maybe a friend or family member gave you this book. Regardless, it is no accident you are here. It is a well-planned event and opportunity for you. Just stay open and pray for truth as you read. If Christ really is the Truth (John 14:6), He will reveal Himself to you in the pages of this book as we talk about Him and His teaching. If He's not, He won't. I'm banking He will. He's amazing at that. Years ago, I walked through this process from not believing to believing. I wasn't raised in a Christian home and didn't even set foot in a church or hear about Jesus until I was twelve. He showed me Who He was and is—and Who He is to me personally—so I could become.

If you've never read Scripture or maybe haven't in a very long time, I want to encourage you to read the Bible. The Gospel of John or the Book of Romans make great starting places to explore this faith. I have provided a basic fact sheet about a relationship with Jesus in the back of this book on Page 233. Go there anytime, should you want to know more. If you decide to become a Christ follower, just let someone know. Maybe the person that gave you this book. Maybe a buddy that you know is a Christian or someone in your life that you see is following Jesus already.

If I were sitting there with you right now, it would be cool to pray for you or with you, but this is as close as we're going to get for now, so ...

*Heavenly Father, you are the King, our King. Thank You that You make it possible for us to not just believe, but to become. Thank You that Your Spirit gives us the tools to put faith into action. Thank You that the challenge of living pure, speaking truth, and righting wrong is completely possible because of Your life, Your death, and Your resurrection. Help us to stay open to You throughout these pages and these days ahead to see, hear, and know Your Truth. Amen.*

## DISCUSSION QUESTIONS

1. Discuss Paul's confession in the opening passage—Romans 7:18–20. How do you relate to his words?

2. Do you believe there can actually be a Source for all answers such as Jesus Christ? Why or why not?

3. Regarding the quote on page 9, "Life on the 'back cover side' of the book often looks no different than life on the 'front cover side' of the book"—why are we often inspired by certain books or messages, yet don't allow the truth we hear to change us? What happens? What doesn't happen?

4. Why do you suppose just knowing a truth doesn't actually change you?

5. Why do you think that true life change is so difficult?

6. Do you believe that God is active in your life? Why or why not?

7. How is "becoming" connected to belief?

8. How has claiming to believe truths that aren't actually practiced hurt the cause of Christianity in our culture?

9. Do we really believe that which we don't do? Discuss.

10. On a scale of 1 to 10, how badly do you really want your life to change? (1 being "I don't care at all" to 10 being "My life has to change and I'm ready.")

Close with the prayer from the end of the chapter or your own.

CHAPTER 2

# ARMOR & ACCOLADES

*"A man's got to have a code, a creed to live by, no matter his job."[1]*
—*John Wayne*

In the mid to late 1800s, the author Alfred Lord Tennyson wrote a series of poetry classics about knights, in particular King Arthur and his Knights of the Round Table, entitled *Idylls of the King.* The stories of Arthur and his knights came from cultural legends and many authors had put those to paper, but what became known by some as the Knight's Code was from Tennyson's work entitled *Gareth and Lynette.* Gareth is about to leave home to journey to Camelot in hopes of fulfilling his dream to join the Round Table. He says to his mother, "Follow the Christ the King. Live pure, speak true, right wrong, follow the King. Else, wherefore born?"[2]

To paraphrase in modern English, "To follow Christ, to live pure, speak true, right wrong, and follow the King. If not to live out these ideals, why else was I born?"

So I ask you—as I asked myself years ago—if not for this, why were you born?

## EVERYMAN

Armor. Swords. Shields. Cold steel. Charging horses. Hand to hand combat. Battles. Protecting the king. Protecting the nation.

Serving in the name of God. What's not to love about that? Isn't it funny how just reading these words can create a little testosterone surge in us guys?

Likely now, some images are already in your mind. Maybe a movie you've seen is playing in your head. Something like *A Knight's Tale, King Arthur,* or *First Knight.* Maybe you think of damsels in distress crying out for rescue or fair maidens swooning over a knight who walks by in that killer metal outfit. (Cue ZZ Top's *Sharp Dressed Man.*) Hey, come on, any guy can look buff in that suit, right? Bottom line is these are all inspiring and healthy images for us as men, in a culture that is increasingly devoid of masculine icons, outside of movie super heroes or the occasional pro athlete.

There are actually two well-known aspects of the historic knight. The first one we have touched on thus far in this chapter—the purely physical, visceral level—the man's man, the warrior, the fighter, but then the second goes past the physical images to the character qualities. Bravery. Strength. Justice. Honor. Generosity. Chivalry. On and on.

Being able to focus on the character of the knight causes it not to matter whether you're a man that's 5'6" or 6'6", weighs 145 or 345. Or how tough you are, or if you're a jock or an artist, blue color or white collar, or your ethnicity, age, income, all that. One of the major premises of the Knight's Code is any type, size, age, or make of man can develop these qualities in his life. No man has an edge over another man. It's not about the body, but the heart. It's not about the strength of the arm, but the strength of the soul. That's what Jesus was about and still is and His life is available to every man, every day.

> NO MAN HAS AN EDGE OVER ANOTHER MAN. IT'S NOT ABOUT THE BODY, BUT THE HEART. IT'S NOT ABOUT THE STRENGTH OF THE ARM, BUT THE STRENGTH OF THE SOUL.

*But the LORD said to Samuel, "Do not consider his appearance or his height, … The LORD does not look at the things man looks at. Man looks at the outward appearance, but the LORD looks at the heart." 1 Samuel 16:7 NIV*

## HUMBLE BEGINNINGS

The concept of the knight began around 800 A.D. and by the 11th century had become an accepted and prevalent order of men.[3] Of course, there were knights that were evil and out for themselves, as any group that is comprised of human beings will have. But predominantly over time, knights gained reputations for virtues such as justice and honor. The overall mission was for these men committed to this station to live out the code of the knight, much like an American soldier is expected to uphold certain values and standards.

Knights vastly improved the attitude towards women by introducing the concept of chivalry, which demanded that ladies be treated with respect and honor.[4] They were to be saved, not savaged. They were to be respected, not ravaged. (I'm sure there are plenty of ladies in the 21st century that would like to see some of that happen today.) Knights were seen, by common people and royalty alike, as a class of men set apart with a high standard of ethics and conduct. They were dedicated to battle and dedicated to the service of the king and God.[5]

There was one group in the 1100s that were known as the Knights Templar. They were a religious order with the status of monks, but were also warriors who fought to protect Christian pilgrims from Muslim attacks. Their quarters were near the Temple in Jerusalem.[6]

## DEATH OF AN ICON

The development of new weapons that could be used by anyone without trained skill led to the eventual demise of the knight. Finally, the introduction of gunpowder sealed the knight's fate. Years of training in swordsmanship and hand-to-hand combat could be useless against a gun fired from a distance where the metal ball or bullet could pierce armor.[7]

With the decline of the knight and the development of weapons that any "layman" could use, it seems the ideals and standards of this medieval icon also fell by the wayside.

This is a very similar process that ended the Western Cowboy era in the U.S. Fences, railroads, motorcars, and industrialization changed forever that American icon. Ironically, there was also a men's creed adopted during that era that later came to be known as *The Code of the West*. That code centered around hospitality, fair play, loyalty, and respect for the land. Note four independent, yet interrelated tenets just as the Knight's Code has. Legendary Cowboy author Zane Grey originated the phrase, "The Code of the West" with his 1934 novel of the same name.[8] For the most part, the rodeo cowboy of today has been able to keep that code alive and intact. The rodeo circuit has a lot of good men. And a strong number of those men follow Jesus.

## A KNIGHT'S PLATE

Fighting and carrying around all that metal probably created quite an appetite. My oldest son has always loved the scenes in many knight movies where they show armored men seated at a huge table eating a dinner of those giant turkey legs. Seems to be the stereotypical Hollywood medieval meal. Sadly today, giant turkey legs have been reduced to "State Fair Food." My son always says, "Man, they make those things look so good. It makes me so hungry!" That's generally where we pause the movie for he and his brother to go get a snack. … But what a great guy image! Gynormous fire-roasted turkey legs. No forks. No napkins. Just fingers. Really gross, greasy fingers! And it is commonly known that knights allowed their dogs to hunt for crumbs under the table, mainly so they could wipe their hands on the dogs as they passed back and forth at their legs. How clever these guys were! (If by chance, a woman started reading this book, I bet I just lost her.)

## A Knight's Prayer

Honoring and serving God was an integral part of the life of many knights. At the Chartres Cathedral in France, a knight's prayer is carved in stone there. It reads: *"Most Holy Lord, Almighty Father, Thou hast permitted on earth the use of the sword to repress the malice of the wicked and defend justice; who for the protection of Thy people hast thought fit to institute the order of chivalry. Cause Thy servant here before Thee, by disposing his heart to goodness, never to use this sword or another to injure anyone unjustly, but let him use it always to defend the just and right."* [9]

Now, if that kind of prayer doesn't cause the hair on the back of your neck to stand up, maybe it's time to check the expiration date on your Man Card! And considering our tolerant, passive society of men that must speak in politically correct terms, notice he isn't praying that he *never* has to use the sword (and remember, this is a prayer), but rather that, when he *does,* he uses it for defense and righteousness. This knight is assuming that he *will be* using his sword. We'll address this concept in modern-day applications later in *Speak True* and *Right Wrong.*

## Training Days

Many knights started their calling as young boys that were trained through an apprenticeship program, where at around the age of seven, they left their families and became a servant to a veteran knight.[10] What a great concept! Actually hanging out with the person you want to be like. Study the life of the one who you yourself want to become. Sounds a bit like discipleship, eh? A lot like Jesus' statement, "Come and follow me and I will make you fishers of men."

There is a great scene depicting the beginning of a boy's journey to knighthood in the movie *A Knight's Tale.*[11] It shows a loving father giving up his son to a knight for training and the promise of a better life, knowing he might never see him again. A very real moment many fathers and mothers experienced during that period. (We will look deeper at this concept in Chapter 4.)

Throughout his adolescent and teen years, there were stages for the knight in training to master various skills before moving forward. I'm not going to take the time to walk through those stages here, because the intention of this book is to get to your own practical and spiritual applications of the Knight's Code, not to be a historical reference, but if you're interested in learning more of their path and training, you might want to check out a book on knights. That might be a good father-son thing to do in looking at the stages of a young knight.

## THE VIGIL

Often, a young knight-to-be would spend the night before his dubbing in a prayer vigil. He was to pray and meditate on the seriousness of his vows of service.[12] (You can Google *The Vigil* by John Pettie for a cool image of a knight praying at the altar during his vigil. Note in the painting where his armor is lying. There's an awesome spiritual picture for you, ala Romans 12:1.)

What if all young ministers today were required to spend the night before an ordination on his knees before the Father, considering the lifestyle he is about to take on? Then what if he had to recite a code or creed of what he would uphold for Christ all his days? Wow! What might that change? That goes a bit deeper than changing Social Security status and securing a profession.

What if all our young Christian men had to go through this process in their church somewhere between the ages of 18 and 21? Think they'd know when they became men according to their family and the church? You think they might take their walk, their purity, and their commitment to God more seriously?

## THE ACCOLADE

When the elder knight believed his protégé was well trained in battle and life, he then deemed him to be ready for knighthood. The young knight would experience a dubbing ceremony, also called an accolade, the origination of our word for praise and recognition. This was most often considered a religious service much like a baptism or ordination. A typical knighting ceremony would involve the elder knight and a bishop. The bishop would bless the various pieces of armor and weaponry as he handed it to the elder knight to place on the young knight. His sword was blessed and used for the final blessing, or the dubbing. Sometimes the person performing the dubbing would be a government official or member of the nation's royalty, with the elder knight and bishop looking on.[13]

Queen Elizabeth still holds dubbing ceremonies today for England to recognize men in their contribution to her nation and the world. In keeping with the origin of knighting, the men recognized by the Queen are nominated for their leadership qualities, humanitarian efforts, and contributions to mankind. What a great tradition to honor men in this historic and masculine manner.

In the knight's accolade, he would have to recite the rules of chivalry and swear a sacred oath that he would uphold the code of the knight all his days. A great sample of a knight's oath can be found in some of the on-line trailers for the movie *Kingdom of Heaven*.[14] (The trailers are PG-rated.)

Here are just a few of the common points of a knight's oath:

      To be generous
      Pursue glory
      Disregard pain, fatigue, and threat of death
      To use the sword only in good causes
      To defend the Holy Church against infidels
      Protect widows, orphans, and the poor
      Help anyone in distress[15]

## CODE OF CHIVALRY

1.  Thou shalt believe all that the church teaches and shall obey all her commandments.
2.  Thou shalt defend the church.
3.  Thou shalt respect all weaknesses and shalt constitute thyself the defender of them.
4.  Thou shalt love the country in which thou wast born.
5.  Thou shalt not recoil before thine enemy.
6.  Thou shalt make war against the infidel without cessation and without mercy.
7.  Thou shalt perform scrupulously thy feudal duties, if they be not contrary to the laws of God.
8.  Thou shalt never lie, and shalt remain faithful to thy pledged word.
9.  Thou shalt be generous, and give largesse to everyone.
10. Thou shalt be everywhere and always the champion of the Right and the Good against injustice and evil.

— Leon Gautier, *The Decalogue*[16]

Read any of the New Testament lately? Do any of these concepts sound familiar? Remind you of Peter, John, James, and Paul? This well describes their lives, doesn't it?

Tie those concepts to this passage of Scripture.

*And now, O Israel, what does the* Lord *your God ask of you but to fear the* Lord *your God, to walk in all his ways, to love him, to serve the* Lord *your God with all your heart and with all your soul, and to observe the* Lord*'s commands and decrees that I am giving you today for your own good? ... For the* Lord *your God is God of gods*

> THOU SHALT BE EVERY-WHERE AND ALWAYS THE CHAMPION OF THE RIGHT AND THE GOOD AGAINST INJUSTICE AND EVIL.

*and Lord of lords, the great God, mighty and awesome, who shows no partiality and accepts no bribes. He defends the cause of the fatherless and the widow, and loves the alien, giving him food and clothing. And you are to love those who are aliens, for you yourselves were aliens in Egypt. Fear the LORD your God and serve him. Hold fast to him and take your oaths in his name.* —Deuteronomy 10:12–13, 17–20 NIV

Hopefully, as you have read through what we have covered thus far, you can now see the alliances between the knights of olde and the men of God. The training of a young knight connects to boys being raised in the church as they come to understand what Christ has done for them and give their lives to Him. As they grow up, they go into training—discipleship—from elder Christian men. Then finally, enter the world to begin their calling and fight their own "battles."

Our best Biblical ideals and concepts of what a male follower of Christ looks like is matched up well with the image of the knight. And I don't know about you, but I need all the help and inspiration I can get! That is a major goal of this book. I believe any image, movie, article, web site, teaching, or personal talk that will motivate and inspire us to grow and change into Christ's image is a good thing. The knight is a strong, positive, motivating icon to challenge us to live a life devoted to the Eternal King—Jesus.

Let's pray: *Heavenly Father, I want to step up and be the man You intend me to be. I don't want to fit anyone else's mold, but I want to conform to Your image. I want to be generous, pursue Your glory, to use my life only in Your causes, to help lead Your church, to protect widows, orphans, and the poor, and to help anyone in distress. When You look at me, I want You to know I am both Your friend and servant. In Christ's name. Amen.*

## DISCUSSION QUESTIONS

1.   Discuss the opening quote from John Wayne. How can a code or creed be helpful to us as men?

2.   Why are we still inspired today by the images and stories of the knight, whether it be in a movie or a book?

3.   Share some parallels you see between the life and commitments of a knight and the Christian man of today.

4.   Do you believe most men struggle with understanding why they are born and for what purpose they are here? Why or why not?

5.   Do you think our culture struggles with positive masculine images? Why or why not?

6.   Read the bold insert statement on Page 19. Discuss.

7.   Why would/could it be a positive for the Knight's Code to be attainable and available to every man?

8.   Discuss the "Code of Chivalry" on Page 25 and the relationship to Scripture.

9.   What are some ways we can live out Number 10 today (p. 25)?

10.  Referring to Deuteronomy 10:12–13, 17–20 (pp. 25–26), what are some ways that we as men today can "fear the Lord, walk in his ways, love him, and serve him with all your heart and soul?"

Close with the prayer at the end of the chapter or pray in your own words.

CHAPTER 3

# I'M *NOT* OKAY, YOU'RE *NOT* OKAY

*"I'm starting with the man in the mirror.*
*I'm askin' if he'll change his ways."* [1]
*—Michael Jackson, early 1988 (prior to any allegations)*

How many times on a typical Sunday morning are you involved in this scenario? You're walking into church and see a guy heading toward you that you know really well—at church—and you say, "Hey, man. How's it going?" He says, "Awesome, man. How are you?" You say, "Doing great." So he says, "Alright, hope you have a great week! See ya." Walking away, you say, "Yeah, man. You too." … One of our deepest, most endearing guy phrases: "You too."

Ahhh … nothing like Christian brothers living life together in the hallways and foyers of our churches, huh? Does it get any better than this? For far too many of us, it doesn't.

Now, let's dive below that surface and ask some questions.

How many men do you know that would really stand up to evil today?

How many men do you know that won't look the other way, but rather will stare evil in the face until it backs down?

A little bit deeper now:

When was the last time you invited a brother into your life to help you walk with God?

When was the last time you confessed sin to a brother and asked for help to stop?

When was the last time you got into a brother's business and asked him how he was really doing in his walk with God?

## IF'S & BUT'S

Years ago I went on a mission trip with about 25 people to a third world country. The group was mixed, male and female, married and single, but very few had their spouse with them on the trip. We were often in cramped quarters and piled into small trucks going here and there. I began to notice a young pastor who was always positioned next to an attractive, young college student. Toward the end of the trip, I even noticed one truck ride where she sat on his lap, because we were very crowded. Now, if you've ever been on a third world mission trip, you know you bond with the people you're with in unique ways and everyone is thinking about ministry and what God is doing, which is exactly where your head and heart are supposed to be. But …

Once we returned home, what I had witnessed started to sink in and concern me, so I talked to a close friend about it that was on the trip and who knew the pastor better than I did. I wanted to find out if he thought I was crazy or did he notice what I had? Well, he *had* noticed it. Our discussion ended with these thoughts: The guy was a pastor, for crying out loud! He was a man of God who led his church and taught the Word. We decided it was all very innocent and we shouldn't do anything. In fact, we might even be a bit perverted for even thinking something might not be right there. We gave him the proverbial "benefit of the doubt" and let it go.

Several months later that young pastor had to resign from his church, because he had an affair. Not with the young lady on the trip, but another one. His pattern was established and he kept up until someone gave in. What I had witnessed was a man on the hunt. But I looked the other way. I ignored the obvious. I let injustice stare me down. And, worst of all, I let a brother down. I chose to ignore and not help him. I believe they call that a sin of omission—I should have done the right thing, but I didn't. Yeah, the pastor sinned, but so did I. Both of us fell short.

But you might say, *"Wait a second, Robert, aren't you being kind of tough on yourself? After all, he had an adulterous affair and all you did was not talk to him?"* … Let me ask you—do you really think God looks at that differently? As much as we'd love to think so, it ain't so! Disobedience to God has one consequence. We don't get to explain our Church-ianity levels of sin concept to a Holy God. "God, my sin was a two, but his was at least a nine, so I'm good, right?" … Omission. Commission. It's all the same to Him. But, thank God that He is just and righteous, yet merciful and gracious.

## TAKE A KNEE, SON

God sat me down and talked to me about that situation. He said, "Son, I show you these things for a reason. I give you discernment for a reason. I allow you to see things others miss and give you that red flag that goes up in your heart for a reason. The next time you get that sense, you act on it, you do what I tell you, you don't ever again just sit on it, don't just "give the benefit of the doubt." If I show you something, don't let anyone—including yourself—talk you out of it. Sure, you may offend someone, but you just might save a life, or a marriage, or a family … or all three!"

*And you have forgotten that word of encouragement that addresses you as sons: "My son, do not make light of the Lord's discipline, and do not lose heart when he rebukes you, because the Lord disciplines those he loves, and he punishes everyone he accepts as a son." Endure hardship as discipline; God is treating you as sons. For what son is not disciplined by his father? —Hebrews 12:5–7 NIV*

That's one of the primary ways we learn. And just to make dead sure that you, as the reader, understand what I'm saying, I'm not talking about the pastor's discipline, but my own. My discipline for ignoring what God had shown me.

And how arrogant we can be when we have sensed something about someone and then when they fall, we get all self-righteous and think, "Yep, I was right all along. I knew there was something funny about him." Where does that attitude get anyone? A brother falls and we get to feel smug and "holy" for a few minutes. Wow, some great stuff for the glory of the Kingdom there, huh? That is all too often an American church mindset and not even in the ballpark with Biblical.

So what if I had obeyed the voice of God and had gone to the pastor after our trip? What if I said, "Hey, brother, I am not coming to sound 'holier than thou' or that I'm any better than you, because I don't know your heart and I certainly blow it myself all the time, but I saw you do some things on that trip that concerned me. I saw you do some things that I'll bet had your wife been there, you wouldn't have done. I'll bet had someone got out a camera and started taking shots for the church slide show, you would have done a little shifting, huh? Is there anything here you need to take a look at? Are you struggling with temptation? You sure don't have to talk to me, but maybe you should talk to someone."

What might that have changed? … I'll never know. And, what's worse, he'll never know.

## Missing in Action

In the late '80s, there seemed to be a spike in the number of sex and/or money scandals among high profile Christian ministers. The last several years have brought yet another round plastered across the media. If you have been inside evangelical Christian circles for even a short time, you likely can name a list of ministers who once had huge followings, but lost them due to a moral failure. If you're Catholic, there are a number of instances with high-level priests that the Church has had to deal with in recent years as well. (I have chosen to intentionally not offer any names here.) If you take a look at this now very long list, what might be some common threads you would see?

Now, I'm not going to go where you think I might with this subject matter. That's been done way too much. The church and the media have dissected these situations, the problems, and the restoration
or lack of, on both printed and digital pages for years.

Here's my question. Let's look not at these men, but around them.
Were there men in these ministers' lives who were speaking truth to
them? Was someone seeing what was going on and trying to deal with
it? Did these men ignore other men who were trying to love them,
speak truth, save their lives and ministries? Maybe. But maybe not.

Now, allow me to pose the question that is the point of this chapter. What if there were men that had a shot at speaking truth and
decided that these ministers were too big, too important, too godly to
be approached? Did God tell any brothers to go to them, but they got
intimidated and decided to look the other way? Are there guys living
with regret today, because they watched this happen and did nothing?

As I have experienced the Christian culture and the church at
large over these last few decades, I can't help but think the answer to
these questions might be yes. Men sensed they should do something,
but then didn't. Why do I assume that? Because if we can't develop
and maintain transparent, caring relationships among the average
men's group in our churches, what makes us think these high profile
guys have any shot? In fact, the more power and wealth a man attains,
the less likely someone will get in their face. As guys, we know that.

As in the scenario I told you about with the pastor on the mission trip, I am not saying these well-known ministers were simply
victims of our Christian culture. No, they blew it and hurt many,
but I am asking this: how many of these prominent Christian leaders, along with countless Christian brothers, would have avoided a
moral failure had another brother had the guts to intervene when
they saw signs of trouble?

*Then Nathan said to David, "You are the man! This is what the
LORD, the God of Israel, says: 'I anointed you king over Israel, and I de-*

*livered you from the hand of Saul. I gave your master's house to you, and your master's wives into your arms. I gave you the house of Israel and Judah. And if all this had been too little, I would have given you even more. Why did you despise the word of the LORD by doing what is evil in his eyes?*
—*2 Samuel 12:7–9a NIV*

We don't like Nathans in this culture. We work hard to get them out of our lives and our churches. But God has a purpose for Nathans. Just ask David when he couldn't seem to correct his life that had spun out of control.

British statesman Edmund Burke said, "Nobody made a greater mistake than he who did nothing because he could only do little."[2]

So you may say, *"Okay, Robert, I see the point and I see the possibility, but what does that have to do with me?"* Simply this: Would you consider being the kind of man that on a regular basis would open his life up to other men for accountability (account for and explain your actions for the purpose of spiritual growth) and to love enough that you would risk relationship and reputation to help another man?

> WOULD YOU CONSIDER BEING THE KIND OF MAN TO LOVE ENOUGH THAT YOU WOULD RISK RELATIONSHIP AND REPUTATION TO HELP ANOTHER MAN?

*Better is open rebuke than hidden love. —Proverbs 27:5 NIV*

I can tell you since that conversation between God and I many years ago (well, He did most of the talking) about the pastor's situation I ignored, I have been much more careful to pay attention and listen when He speaks those warnings to me.

## RISK, RELATIONSHIP, & REPUTATION

Now, if you're considering this at all, there are four scenarios you must understand that come with the territory, because there is a risk factor. I will speak from personal perspective and experience.

First, I have totally missed God. I have gotten it all wrong. I've misinterpreted circumstances and had to apologize for assuming wrong. I had cause for question, but got all the right answers from the person.

The second is that I've been right, but handled it all wrong. I've pushed too hard and offended. I didn't apply enough grace. So, in short, I did the right thing the wrong way. Did a Jesus thing in a non-Jesus fashion. Right motive, wrong action.

Third, I've been right, handled it right, but gotten my hand bit badly and my name dragged through the mud from someone who wasn't about to let me into his situation or deal with his issue. He just went into defensive attack mode. Many men will let you walk through their house, but just won't open certain doors. That is going to happen. You are just going to lose those battles. But, unfortunately, guess which one loses the war? The one who won't deal with their issue and allow a brother to help. That is painful.

But here's the fourth and final scenario. I've been right. Handled it right. I heard from the Lord and obeyed. And the brother responded by doing exactly what he needed to do and took care of what he needed to take care of under the submission and authority of the Holy Spirit, Who was already at work in his heart. There is nothing quite like one man telling another, "Thank you for loving me enough to get in my business and risk the relationship. I needed someone to do this." That is joyful.

Bottom line: A man's life and witness is worth the risk we must take, because that man is important to God and His Kingdom.

*Therefore confess your sins to each other and pray for each other so that you may be healed. —James 5:16a NIV*

So, loving your brothers on this level involves risk, commitment, time, and energy. Love has to ultimately be the motivation. Not some kind of personal spiritual glory, or an opportunity to be demeaning in the name of God, or to get another Christian merit badge. It can't be like a touchdown scored in high school that you talk about until you're 45. This has to become a lifestyle, if we are going to change the current climate inside and outside the church for men.

Now, a really curious aspect of this issue is that some men will applaud you for confronting another man with truth. They will high five you and tell you how awesome they think it is that you would do that. But … if you try it with them, well, see Scenario #3 again. … They're like the guys who love watching the crotch hits on *America's Funniest Home Videos.* It's a real hoot to watch someone else get nailed, but nobody better laugh if they get racked.

## WE WILL ALL COME HOME TOGETHER

God wants us all to cross His finish line. He wants us to choose some brothers whom we will take care of and they will take care of us. He wants everyone to be on His team. He wants us to love each other, honor one another, and do what it takes to help each other stand strong and grow in Him.

Harold "Hal" Moore, Jr. was the Lieutenant Colonel in command of the First Battalion, 7th Calvary Regiment at the Battle of la Drang in 1965 during the Viet Nam War. His book, *We Were Soldiers Once … and Young* was made into a movie entitled *We Were Soldiers* with Mel Gibson cast to play Lt. Colonel Moore.[3] Before his Battalion left for Viet Nam, he shared the following speech with his men: *"I can't promise you that I will bring you all home alive. But this I swear, before you and before Almighty God, that when we go into battle, I will be the first to set foot on the field, and I will be the last to step off, and I will leave no one behind. Dead or alive, we will all come home together. So help me, God."*[4]

This is exactly the kind of brotherhood and commitment I'm talking about.

So, you got a "Hal Moore" in your life?

Are you a "Hal Moore" to anyone?

Do you have a group of guys that have decided you will all be committed to help each other get home together? Are you committed to Christ and to each other's lives to the point that you would risk relationship and reputation to make sure that each one walks the narrow path and stays strong in their faith to the very end?

*Put on the full armor of God so that you can take your stand against the devil's schemes. For our struggle is not against flesh and blood, but against the rulers, against the authorities, against the powers of this dark world and against the spiritual forces of evil in the heavenly realms. Therefore put on the full armor of God, so that when the day of evil comes, you may be able to stand your ground, and after you have done everything, to stand. —Ephesians 6:11–13* NIV

Scriptures like this in the New Testament are clear that the closer we walk with Christ and the more serious we take our faith and service to God, the more intense the battle we will walk in daily. Speaking in spiritual metaphor, we do not know when we will find ourselves right smack in the middle of our own "Battle of la Drang" in our own "Viet Nam."

Some of you reading this already know about spiritual warfare. You got up one morning, just minding your own business and, without warning, all Hell broke loose in your life. Suddenly you were in enemy territory and surrounded, the odds stacked against you. Some of you had your God and your brothers in place and won. It was a tough fight, but you eventually saw victory.

Those who were alone and defenseless lost the battle. You may still be trying to recover.

And some of you reading this may feel absolutely dead on the battlefield from a spiritual perspective, because you have become a casualty in this heavenly war we are in. Victorious and standing or broken and defeated, please keep your head up and keep reading.

## IF YOU WENT TOO FAR …

Regardless of where you are, answer these:

Who has your back?
Who would risk for you?
If you went too far, who would go get you?
and …
Whose back do you have?
Who would you risk for?
Who would you walk through Hell to get back?

As a Christian man, these are vitally important questions to answer. Maybe you should get a group of buddies together and ask each other these questions. Maybe you should give a few brothers permission now to do these things, should the need arise *later*. And let me tell you, it will arise. It's not if, but when.

If after you share this with your Christian buddies, they tell you they're all in, then just get after being brothers to each other. The rest of this book will help you formulate a plan.

If your buddies aren't interested in taking this on with you, then maybe it's time to find some guys who will. Stay friends with those guys and pray for them. Or it could be time to get some new friends. Why? This is important stuff in the Kingdom. That's why. This is about making sure you get to the end of your life, not just making it to Heaven, but experiencing major wins for Christ's Kingdom and doing damage to the enemy's camp. And helping your buddies do the same. … Remember Gareth's question: If not for this, why else was I born?

You don't write a will and buy life insurance when you're on your deathbed. You have to plan in advance for that moment. You can't pull life together in those last breaths. Why? Because you rarely know when that will occur. … Well, you rarely plan on getting blindsided and schedule a moral fall either! So, get a plan now. God forbid you ever use it, but what if it saves your life some day when you least expect it? What if you save the life of a buddy, because the plan was agreed on by both of you?

Consider these statements:

- – A knight didn't look the other way. A Christian brother shouldn't either.
- – A knight would risk offense for the sake of justice. So should a Christian brother.
- – A knight would challenge a man to get to the truth. So should a Christian brother.

Consider these Scriptures:

*My dear friends, if you know people who have wandered off from God's truth, don't write them off. Go after them. Get them back and you will have rescued precious lives from destruction and prevented an epidemic of wandering away from God. —James 5:19–20* MSG

*Love from the center of who you are; don't fake it. Run for dear life from evil; hold on for dear life for good. Be good friends who love deeply. —Romans 12:9–10a* MSG

Isn't it time we got back to the simple rules of brotherhood? What are we afraid of? Vulnerability? Rejection? Gossip? Political correctness? Church-ical correctness?

## Don't Make Me Come Over There

Scanning history, how have men taken care of a conflict with another guy? Well, there's sword fights. Jousting. Hand to hand combat. Pistol duels. Gun fights in the street. Fist fights in the alley.

And then there's the issues that occur today between men within the average American church. I can hear the ref now: "Okay, you boys go home and talk about each other to your wives. Tell your wives all the stuff you're never going to really say to the other guy's face. Then hold it in, don't deal with it, and don't forgive. Ready. Go!"

Please don't misunderstand, I am not advocating we re-instate pistol duels. (It has crossed my mind a few times, but …) I know as believers we are not supposed to hurt each other in any manner. But I am asking the question: Why have we become such a polarized population of men where when a man fails or offends, we either make the choice of destroying a brother behind his back and avoiding the guy or acting like nothing ever happened and ignoring his obvious need? Ignoring the guy or ignoring his need. Really, either of these choices are cowardice and un-Biblical. There is a place of Biblical balance that both Jesus and all the New Testament writers instructed us in that falls correctly in between sword throwing and backstabbing (We'll deal with conflict in the *Speak True* and *Right Wrong* chapters.)

We must understand that, as brothers, we will fail each other. We will say stupid things to each other. We will be incredibly insensitive to one another. We will let each other down. We're guys AND we're sinners! What an amazingly scary combination! But if we admit we know this going in, and we are committed to Christ and to each other, then we deal with conflict as the Scriptures teach and move on. We will all learn and grow. There is not a single scenario that a man would face today that the Scriptures do not offer a practical principle and solution for. We will constantly see that throughout this book.

## Ministry is Messy

Several years ago when we were leaving our first church start to plant our second and final one, one of the young couples we were very close to, decided that, rather than stay with the first plant or start the new one with us, they needed to go to a larger church that had more to offer. They handled it properly in communicating with us and we totally understood. We would miss them, but we blessed their departure. All good.

About two years later and after the birth of their first child, his wife caught him in an affair and a web of pornography addiction. Let's just say it hit the fan. … Meanwhile, back at their new church, they were committed, engaged, tithing, and active in a small group. Exactly the kind of church members you want. But guess what? … The pastor never called. The church ignored them. The husband went to their small group to get the story straight and dispel the rumors, to confess his sin, ask forgiveness, and ask for support for his grieving wife. The small group listened to his story, said little, he left, and no one from that group ever even contacted either of them again.

He came to me and she came to my wife and asked for help. And I'm grateful to say that over time and through Hell and high … well, more Hell, they made it and are a thriving, committed couple today with *two* children.

To get there, here's some stuff that had to happen that most Christians and churches don't want to deal with, as was displayed in their "home church": unplugging and hauling away computers, sitting with him while he called the "girlfriend" to break it off, listening to her scream and cuss and cry, intercepting e-mails from her until they stopped, sitting knee to knee with the couple and airing every issue, "throwing up" years of secrets, dealing with sexual dysfunction, financial issues. … Should I go on? Get the picture? The healing and restoration process took a LOT of time, energy, prayer, and grace for all four of us.

Out of so many situations like this, my wife and I coined a phrase: Ministry is messy.

When you dive into the toilet with people, you are going to get crap on you. It's a given. And it stinks. Not easy. Not what you signed up for. Zero glory. Not how you build a mega-church. And you can't let people know what you're doing, because the matter is so sensitive and confidential. But … here's the other side …

That couple is now at another small church as lay leadership and you know the coolest thing? I guarantee you that the first time a marriage around them falls, our friends will not shut the door, or ignore, or look the other way, or gossip. They will fly into action and duplicate the grace and mercy they were given. They will replicate the process they walked through and be a part of someone else's restoration. They will get someone else's crap on them. It will stink. Not easy. Not what they signed up for. Zero glory. Not how you build a mega-church. And they won't be able to tell anyone, because it's sensitive and confidential.

Ministry is messy. But they learned that … by experience.

I share this story to bring home the major point, along with the close of this chapter. We have a problem in this American Christian culture of being hearers of the Word and not doers. … (James 1:22–23) I repeat—We have a problem in this American Christian culture of being hearers of the Word and not doers. So many want the title of leader, but don't want to serve people. Serving people meaning the level of time and energy commitment I described in the couple's story. We have a problem when our little Christian fantasy worlds of perfection can't handle the truth of someone's reality show sin.

> WE HAVE A PROBLEM WHEN OUR LITTLE CHRISTIAN FANTASY WORLDS OF PERFECTION CAN'T HANDLE THE TRUTH OF SOMEONE'S REALITY SHOW SIN.

The couple in my story—their small group closed the door on my hurting, broken friend and finished their #@!*%^# Bible study! The reality of Scripture walked in their door and they responded with, "No, thank you. We're too busy studying to actually do anything." … What's that about?! Do I hear the sound of a resounding gong or a clanging cymbal? Yes, I believe I do!

This story is a great example of a rampant, systemic problem. This story is repeated over and over inside and outside the church on a regular basis. So, what do we do about it?

## IN YOUR COURT

I am all too aware that I have spent an entire chapter outlining a problem. My reasoning is I want you to be fully aware of WHY we as Christian brothers need:

— a simple Biblical code to live by

— a fresh challenge to be 21st century New Testament disciples

— and new inspiration to leave the bleachers and get back out on the field. Not the sidelines, the field!

With the next chapter, we're going to begin talking about answers. I didn't enjoy writing what I said in this chapter, because I abhor presenting problems with no solutions. My college degree was in business, not ministry. I know you don't operate a successful organization without real functioning solutions. And God wired us guys to solve problems. Then there's an unfortunate hyper-group of us that can't rest until we do.

I fully realize I painted the church with a broad brush in this chapter, outlining the tendencies of many churches and the prevailing religiousness and legalism that divides us. But that's over now in this book. From this point forward, I want to warn you that the solutions I will offer will only involve you. If you want me to put the responsibility on your church, your pastor, denomination, the government, or whatever, sorry, we're going to be talking practical application for you. Primarily because YOU are the one reading this book and YOU are ultimately responsible before God for your actions.

The problem is not "the world," or church leadership, or even women. It's men. Period. And I am one. The leadership of the church rests on our shoulders. The future of the faith rests on our decisions. The integrity of the Gospel rests on our level of obedience.

## Live Tough, Think Big

So, guys, what about instead of acting tough and talking big, we tried to live tough and think big? For the Christian man, we certainly have all we need to accomplish this. We follow Jesus. … yeah, I believe dying on a cross and changing the world qualifies for both living tough and thinking big, don't you? That's why *really* following Him is not easy. In fact, most days, it's just flat out hard. Making sure we all get home together is a tough commitment. Accepting personal responsibility for the Kingdom is a brave task. Ministry is messy.

In the movie *The Guardian* with Kevin Costner and Ashton Kutcher, Costner plays a seasoned veteran Coast Guard rescuer and Kutcher plays the young, arrogant trainee, Jay. Throughout the movie, the recruits have tried to find out the Senior's "number," meaning the number of people he had rescued in his career. There were only rumors of how high his number was because he would never tell anyone.

Near the end of the movie, Kutcher's character asks his trainer (Costner) before he leaves to retire, "Senior, before you go, I gotta know one thing. What's your real number?" Costner hesitates and then says, "22." Kutcher looks surprised and disappointed, then says, "22. That's not bad. It's not 200, but …" Costner interrupts, "22's the number of people I lost, Jay. It's the only number I kept track of."[5]

There's a strong principle for us to learn here, gentlemen.

*If I speak in the tongues of men and of angels, but have not love, I am only a resounding gong or a clanging cymbal. If I have the gift of prophecy and can fathom all mysteries and all knowledge, and if I have a faith that can move mountains, but have not love, I am nothing. If I give all I possess to the poor and surrender my body to the flames, but have not love, I gain nothing.*

*And now these three remain: faith, hope and love. But the greatest of these is love.* —1 Corinthians 13:1–3, 13 *NIV*

Let's pray: *Lord God, You know more than anyone that our sin nature wants us to blame others and deflect personal responsibility. Father, help me to begin to take responsibility for my brother's well-being. Show me the men in my life that need me. Show me the brothers that I need to submit my heart to. Let me know what it's like to look into a band of brothers' eyes and know we are all going to get home together. It is only by Your grace and mercy that we can live this life and make it home. We honor You and Your life in us. In the name of the King, Amen.*

## DISCUSSION QUESTIONS

1.  As guys, why do we tend to stay "on the surface" with each other?

2.  Talk about the man you respect the most in your life and explain why. (Names aren't necessary.)

3.  Discuss the three questions under the text "A little bit deeper now" at the bottom of Page 28 and top of Page 29.

4.  Why do you think our culture has turned more and more to "looking the other way," rather than dealing with issues head-on?

5.  Discuss the question on Page 33: "Would you consider being the kind of man to love enough that you would risk relationship and reputation to help another man?"

6.  Read the Hal Moore story on Page 35. Discuss the questions below the story.

7.  Discuss the questions at the top of Page 37 under the heading *If You Went Too Far.*

8.  Read and discuss the story from *The Guardian* movie on Pages 42–43.

Take the rest of your time discussing how you can best help each other in your faith and to stand strong in your walk with God. Get a practical plan of how to help each other, not just for a few weeks, but for many years.

Close with the prayer at the end of the chapter or pray your own.

CHAPTER 4

# DEALING WITH DAD, FACING THE FATHER

*"Every generation blames the one before, and all*
*of their frustrations come beating on your door."* [1]
—*Mike & the Mechanics*

If you are a male, then you are a father's son. (How's that for stating the obvious?) Being a son may have been and still is a major blessing to you or it could be one of the most painful experiences of your life. Possibly it has been both, in either order. A childhood relationship that was great, until some event turned everything very wrong, or a dad you may not have known for some reason and something later turned your hearts toward each other.

This chapter will consist of two parts. The first is a portion of my personal testimony that involves my dad and my life as a son. I want you to better understand where I'm coming from and my motivation in writing this book for men. Hearing the "fires of life" that a man has walked through, helps us understand where he has come from to better know where he is trying to go—and take you.

My testimony will set up the second part of this chapter. It is something I had to deal with in a major way in my own life, and especially after being in ministry over these many years, have come to realize that most men must face as well. It is a spiritual exercise that could potentially be very powerful for you in dealing with your past and present, as well as vastly change your future. This is the first of many practical applications we will walk through.

But first, here's a part of my story …

## PROBLEMS & PLACIDYLS

As long as I can remember, my father suffered from what is now known as Bi-polar Disorder. (Back in the day, it was known as manic depression.) As I got older, he became worse. Some of my earliest childhood memories were of visiting him in the hospital, but knowing he wasn't sick in the way most people in the hospital were sick. Something else was wrong. I could see the fear in my father's eyes and hear the uncertainty in his voice. He struggled with mental, emotional, spiritual, and eventually physical issues for most of his adult life. And, I don't mean this to be disrespectful, just factual, but he was his own worst enemy. No one could make my father's life worse than my father.

Raised on a small farm in rural Texas poverty, he went to school and worked the land with his family, but learned the guitar for entertainment. As he got older, he started singing and playing in public. By the time he was around 20, music became his ticket out and soon the farm was in his rear-view mirror. It wasn't long before he was able to start making his living as a musician. He became what was known back then as a "front man" in country music. The front man typically played rhythm guitar, sang lead vocals, and handled all the banter in between songs to entertain the crowd. He was also the most likely one to get hit with a flying beer bottle, because he was the easiest target for a drunken music critic.

By the early '50s, my dad was playing for a traveling show band that also did a live radio program each weekday. They recorded and released a couple of 78's (the first vinyl record format), both to sell to fans and for radio airplay. The band's publicity photos of my dad during that time showed a happy, content entertainer, doing what he loved.

He began to be asked to open shows for country legends like Little Jimmy Dickens and Hank Snow, the George Strait and Alan Jackson's of that day. However, like so many young men in that era, Uncle Sam changed all that with a single letter. He was drafted into the Air Force, just as his career was taking off. … My dad was never quite the same after that.

Life began a very slow downhill journey from there, but downhill nonetheless. Now, fast forward—after meeting and marrying my mom, having their first son deliver still-born, being transferred by the Air Force to the frozen tundra of Alaska, having me there, being discharged after eight years, and then having to make a living being a "phone man," as they use to call it, life was no longer what he had hoped it would be. He was a disillusioned and cynical man. He was a man who now had responsibility, a family, as well as a career that the Air Force had chosen for him, but one he would always regret he didn't change. To be clear, he loved my mom and me, but I don't think he loved life anymore.

By the '60s, the prevalence of prescription drugs was growing and doctors in small towns often found it easier to prescribe pills to mask symptoms, rather than actually deal with the real issues producing the symptoms. Mental and emotional health was something discussed in hushed tones and was not at all a public issue. So, the conversation between doctor and patient became, "Can't sleep, huh? Well, take these an hour before you're ready to go to bed. They're called Placidyls." … "Now, you say you're struggling to wake up and deal with life? Take these to keep you going through your day. They're called Valiums." On the street, they were known as uppers and downers. And that is exactly what they did. Artificially and chemically brought you up and brought you down. This began years of a horribly vicious cycle that entrapped my family in the secret web of addiction. Meanwhile, my dad's spirit was dying, which was the original unaddressed problem to begin with.

When my dad would try and talk to my mom, he was most often met with tears and fears, and understandably so, therefore he decided I was a better candidate for listening. This began when I was around ten to twelve years old. Throughout my adolescent and teen years, a typical night for me was to sit and listen to my dad talk about the same problems he had talked to me about the night before and the night before that and the night before that. This went on for many years. Even when I would stay out too late with my buddies, he would be waiting up for me, not to discuss a violated curfew, but to talk over his issues. I didn't have a lot of time to suffer from normal teen angst, because I had to listen to dad's adult angst. Some of the trouble I was getting myself into didn't compare to the trouble he was in on a daily basis. I heard regularly how he was going to be gone soon and I would "have to be strong for my mom." If I ever tried to reason with him or encourage him to get help, he would just say, "Son, you're just too young to understand. One day when you go into the real world, you'll get to see what I'm talking about."… Makes a young man really look forward to tackling the future, huh?!

My dad's life was dominated by two things: fear and pills.

## THE BEST THAT YOU CAN HOPE FOR

Let me stop here and say I can tell you honestly that I do not have a shred of bitterness or unforgiveness in me regarding my dad anymore. It's always going to hurt and I'll never know what a normal father/son relationship will be like, but I'm good now.

Here's why I'm sharing this: I want you to fully grasp why I'm so passionate about men finding their path in Christ and helping each other. To not just survive, but thrive! I watched my dad die a little every day. I watched him just exist for all of my life. I watched him live in painful isolation, keeping secrets in his own private Hell, and not allowing anyone in. I vowed as a teenager that I would never live that way. But here's where the real corner was turned for me: when I surrendered to Christ and to His calling on my life at 19 years old, I vowed I didn't want _any_ man to live that way—if I could help it. So rather than fall into the trap of misery and carrying on the legacy of my father, I chose to allow the Lord to use it as fuel for change in me, my family, and my ministry. That's the difference only Jesus can bring. Bitterness and forgiveness are both fuels. It's just a matter of which fire they're stoking. We either repeat or repent. Repeat—do again ourselves—the pattern we've been given. Or repent—turn around and change—from the pattern we've been given. It's the difference of who (or Who) we give control of our life to.

> BITTERNESS AND FORGIVENESS ARE BOTH FUELS. IT'S JUST A MATTER OF WHICH FIRE THEY'RE STOKING.

My worldview had to zoom out from my world to God's world. Now that's a big zoom! And that's a lot bigger and better world.

For the ending to my story, you might ask, _"So, Robert, this is a 'Christian book,' so I guess your Dad eventually met Christ, was delivered from the pills, and got it all turned around just like it happens in the perfect Christian world our churches live in? Just like a Hallmark movie ends, right? That's what happened, right?"_ … Sorry, no. The stark reality is my dad overdosed on Placidyls one night when he was only 48 years old and I was just 19. His OD probably was not intentional. … probably. But we'll never know. He likely took a couple and then was just so out of it that he forgot and took more. That's why my mom did a daily pill inventory, to try and avoid what inevitably happened anyway.

A few years later after I went into ministry, I worked on some Christian events with Rick Stanley, Elvis' step-brother who became a Christian, and he told me that Placidyls were a major part of Elvis' nightly regimen too. These are pills that can make horses sleep, folks, so it's fairly easy for men to die taking them.

My dad used to tell me that his favorite line of a song was from Kenny Rogers' hit _The Gambler,_ which said: "And the best that you can hope for is to die in your sleep."[2] Well, that's exactly what my father did. … So I was determined I would find a better line from a better song for me and my two sons. … (No offense, Kenny.)

The draining presence of my father, coupled with his emotional and spiritual absence throughout my childhood, followed by his final departure from my life right at a crucial point in my own manhood, made for some interesting days, especially with no siblings and now a widowed mom.

There is some good news here though, shortly after my father died, my mom came to Christ and was baptized while in her late 40's. Adults in their 40's don't come to Jesus very often. I think my mom watched my life and my dad's and saw the difference in me. When I told her the ONLY difference was Jesus, she got it. After all, I was born my father's son, but I made a decision to become my Father's son through His adoption (Romans 8:23–24).

And that is exactly the point of the next section of this chapter. Now it's your turn.

## FATHER FIGURE

What I am about to share, I want to encourage you to strongly consider, even if you have heard this concept discussed before. Here it is: Our earthly father image greatly affects and molds our Heavenly Father image. As men, we will knowingly or unknowingly, apply the qualities of dad to God. We just do. It's a transference that seems natural, even though it's never correct. It's not always unhealthy, but it can never be completely accurate. Why?

*"Which of you fathers, if your son asks for a fish, will give him a snake instead? Or if he asks for an egg, will give him a scorpion? If you then, though you are evil, know how to give good gifts to your children, how much more will your Father in heaven give the Holy Spirit to those who ask him!" —Luke 11:11–13 NIV*

Even the best dads in the world can't match the love of our Heavenly Father.

Let me give you a few examples of how we confuse God and dad.

If dad was a weak, whipped man, then grasping a God of authority and power is a stretch. That son can struggle with believing God really backs His commands and promises. Dad backs down all the time, so God probably does too.

Conversely, if dad was a heavy-handed taskmaster, then to that son, God can feel like He's looming over with arms crossed and one eyebrow up, just waiting on him to screw up. This is an all too common image of God that is incorrect.

My dad's unspoken motto was "just-tow-the-line-and-we'll-be-fine." As a result, for years I struggled with trying to "perform" for God, so He would approve of my behavior. All the while, thinking He doesn't really want to hear what I have to say. Remember how I said I had to sit and listen to my dad for years? Well, the upside is I have no problem sitting and listening to God speak!

Now, that's the dad side. Here's the son side. We, as men, must realize that we have a choice in how we view God. Yes, we may or may not have baggage from dad, but there is a point where we are solely responsible for carrying dysfunction on and even passing it to the next generation. As Christian men, we can deal with this Biblically, giving it to God, and walking forward in His image.

An exercise I did a few years back has really helped me begin to overcome my inherited patterns and attitudes and has made headway for me to learn God for Who He really is. I wrote all my feelings out on paper—about dad and about God. I was deadly honest with God about what my childhood had created and my feelings of confusion and violation from my dad's choices. Doing that helped process my stuff with my dad out loud and in the open, so it was no longer stuck in and rolling around in my heart and mind. I finally gave the pain an outlet. And when my wife read it, it helped her understand a lot of my personal barriers that I had brought into our marriage, and it helped her help me.

We, as men, often have all this stuff floating around in our minds and hearts that we know is there, but it doesn't quite seem real, because we never deal with it or discuss it. But that's about as effective for your future as trying to ignore a gunshot wound. You're eventually going to bleed to death.

To be perfectly clear, I believe every man should respect and honor his father. That is a Scriptural mandate. I believe if there are unresolved issues or points of contention between father and son, those should be put on the table and discussed and made right. That, too, is a Scriptural mandate. The relationship between a father and son is crucial to both men and that relationship should always be prioritized and made to be the strongest it can be.

But in my years of discipling and counseling men, I have seen consistently how a man's present and future can be completely derailed by his past with his dad. I've talked with so many men who were tough 40-something's, but were still terrified of a now decrepit, dying man—dad. I've seen grown men who are bright and successful believe they were absolute failures, simply because one man never voiced approval—dad. I've watched men wreck marriages and the lives of their children, because they just couldn't shake the image of—dad. I've also had many men sit and blame every current dysfunction they have on—dad.

## WHO'S YOUR DADDY?

You have your own story with your father. I'm certain as you've been reading, that relationship has been playing out in your mind.

Maybe your dad was amazing and awesome—a regular Ward Cleaver and, golly Wally, just super. I really hope so. If that is your situation, what a great picture of God you must have! (I used to watch *Leave It to Beaver* every day at 5 p.m. before my parents would come home from work, always wondering what it would be like to have a dad like Ward. He solved everything in 22 minutes without yelling or anything, and he had Eddie Haskell's number too!)

Or maybe dad was never around. Maybe he left you and mom when you were little. Or maybe he traveled a lot and was just absent from your home. So, with that image, how in the world do you get a grasp on a caring, ever-present Heavenly Father that loves you?

Or maybe dad was just your average American work-a-lot-and-play-sports-some dad, but mom may have run the house and the family and took you to church … sometimes. I'm a child from the '60s and there are a ton of us around like that. ("Don't talk, son, just throw the ball.")

My last example is where far too many of us are at, unfortunately: At some point in your childhood, dad left, he and your mom got a divorce, and you saw him on a scheduled, but irregular basis for the rest of your growing up. What does that paradigm do for understanding an ever-faithful God Who is always there for us?

Regardless of your earthly father image, I'm going to ask you to take a major step before we go on in this book and dig into the Knight's Code. I'm going to ask you to do what I had to do. I'm going to ask you to let go of your earthly dad—whatever he was or wasn't, whether he did or didn't, whether he was the best or the worst, present or absent, whether he dearly loved you or you desperately hated him. I'm asking you now to leave the image of your earthly father and embrace the image of your Heavenly Father.

There is a state you have to commit your heart to where you desire more than anything to allow God to motivate you, mold you, and make you into what He wants. His calling will take priority over dad's expectations. His will for you will take precedent over dad's wishes for your life. God's unchanging character will trump all of dad's earthly imperfections.

Here's why this is necessary for a man and allow me to give you two extreme examples.

Suppose you have a wonderful, healthy dad image. That can actually make some men feel like they don't really need God. They love and respect their father so much that they feel being molded into his image is good enough. Hey! Emulate and copy all of dad's great qualities. Please! But … put God in His rightful place in your life. Allow dad to be dad and God to be God. And, I know you don't want to think about this, but it is likely there will be a day when dad is gone and you will want that deep relationship with your Heavenly Father to be able to get through the loss of your earthly dad. Here's the final gauge of where you are on this scenario. Ask yourself: which do you care more about—dad's will or God's will?

Let's look at the other side of this coin: There is nothing you like about dad. You don't want to be like him in any way. Your harbored feelings are poisoning you. For you, you have to forgive and set him

> YOU MAY BE SO BUSY TRYING TO *NOT* BECOME YOUR DAD, THAT YOU'RE NOT ALLOWING YOUR-SELF TO *BE* GOD'S SON.

and yourself free, so you can begin to become what your Heavenly Father wants. You may be so busy trying to *not* become your dad, that you're not allowing yourself to *be* God's son.

If your story is in between these two extremes, it is likely by now you get the point. The need is there for us all to embrace God. Love dad, honor dad, respect dad, but make sure God is the One Who sits on the throne of your life and is the One Whose approval you seek.

## THE NOD OF THE HEAD

As we stated earlier for a young knight-to-be, at around the age of seven, he was taken to the elder knight and left there by his father to be raised in the ways of the code. The elder knight would teach him how to be a man in every manner—from finances to fighting, from women to weaponry, from reputation to revelry. But the boy had to first leave his father to be under the full authority of the knight. Some never saw their families again, while others were reunited as an adult.

Earlier, I mentioned the scene in the movie *A Knight's Tale* where the young boy named William was handed over by his dad to the knight. Here's some dialogue from that scene:

Elder Knight: (He looks at the dad.) "He's got spirit!" (Now he looks into the eyes of the boy.) "I can show you a great, wide, wonderful world full of adventure and marvels that you wouldn't dream of! Now, say goodbye to your father. Let's get started."

William's dad embraces him and says, "He's a real knight, William! Watch and learn all you can. It's all I can do for you. Now go and change your stars and live a better life than I can."[3]

As William's dad releases him, he looks into the eyes of the knight and there is a very subtle, yet mutual nod of the head. That simple nod was the passing of authority of this young boy's life and future. That simple nod changed William's life forever.

In that day, the end result of a knight's training was often a new creation—an honorable, feared warrior and champion who would defend the poor, women and children, the King, and the name of God.

God wants more than anything to make you into a new creation—an honorable warrior and champion who will defend the poor, women and children, and His name.

*Therefore, if anyone is in Christ, he is a new creation; old things have passed away; behold, all things have become new. —2 Corinthians 5:17 NKJV*

Gentlemen, what I am saying is there is a time to commit to the molding of your life into the image of your Heavenly Father. It is time for you to see the nodding of the head of your King. It is time for the authority of your life to be fully passed to God.

If you are a father of sons, there will be a point where you must, in some manner, embrace your own son and say, "He's a real Savior, son! Watch and learn all you can. It's all I can do for you. Now go and change your stars and live a better life than I can." You too must be certain your son knows He is released to walk into the image of His Heavenly Father.

Even though you may be far from boyhood, this event has to oc-cur for you to grow in and under the authority of Christ. No matter what your situation or how old you are, you have to say goodbye to dad and his image and come over to your Heavenly Father and allow Him to mold you into His image. Your earthly dad conceived and raised you, but your Heavenly Father shaped you in your mother's womb and is now ready to mold your character—who you really are. He wants you to look like Him. He wants to watch you live pure, speak true, right wrong and say, "That's my boy!" He wants to look around when He's changing the world and see you right there beside Him! Because you only follow Him, the King!

Surrendering to God on this level is a major turning point in your spiritual growth. Like salvation, it doesn't matter *when* it happens, but *that* it happens! The nodding of the head.

## UNPACKING BAGGAGE

The decision to move the authority of your life from dad to God is the "what." Now, let's look at the "how."

You have to decide to unpack any emotional and spiritual Dad baggage you may have. There is a time to throw down the gauntlet and let go of what dad did or didn't do, accept the responsibility of your own sin, get it straight with your Heavenly Father, begin to allow Him to rid you of it, and move on in health. You have to talk this stuff out and deal with it. You have to face up to and forgive dad. You have to stop living with dad daily in your own heart and blaming him for you not being/acting like a man now.

For some of you, this is a "10 percent" thing. In other words, there's some stuff you need to deal with, but it's not a major train wreck in your life. Even still, to fully come under the authority of your Heavenly Father, you should take care of that 10 percent now.

For others, this is a "90 percent" thing. If you're 25, 30, 40, even 50 years old and won't step up to the plate and lead in your life, tell me again how that's your dad's fault anymore? That has to stop. You have to end that blaming cycle right now. It has gotten you nowhere but stuck.

Move into the molding and shaping of Christ and His character. Whether you're a "10 percenter" or a "90 percenter," this process can set you free.

*Whenever, though, they turn to face God as Moses did, God removes the veil and there they are—face-to-face! They suddenly recognize that God is a living, personal presence, not a piece of chiseled stone. And when God is personally present, a living Spirit, that old, constricting legislation is recognized as obsolete. We're free of it! All of us! Nothing between us and God, our faces shining with the brightness of his face. And so we are transfigured much like the Messiah, our lives gradually becoming brighter and more beautiful as God enters our lives and we become like him.*
—*2 Corinthians 3:16–18* MSG

## DECLARATION & DELIVERANCE

I want to ask you to pray with me now. Don't just write it off and skip to the next chapter. In fact, often the guys who want to skip this are the very ones who most need to deal with it. This is a spiritual exercise that needs to be dealt with before you can successfully take on the rest of this book.

This needs to be read out loud. This needs to be declared. Get somewhere alone and speak it out. If you need to yell, go for it. God wants to hear it! Satan needs to hear it! You must hear yourself say it! Here we go:

*"Dear Heavenly Father, Abba, Daddy. Thank you for my earthly father. My relationship with him is why I am where I am today. Thank You that he is a part of what brings me to this moment with You. Holy Spirit, please reveal anything to me that I need to face about my father that I may not have seen before. Today, I let go of and forgive anything he did that hurt me—intentional or not—or anything he didn't do that*

*he should have done, that hurt me. I let go of and forgive anything from my father that has hindered me in the past, is dragging me down now, and affecting my future attitude and behavior. I want to move into my future unhindered from my past. From this day forward, my actions will be determined by and responsible to You, Lord, led by Your Spirit. I choose to stand only under the authority of You, my Heavenly Father, by, because of, and through the blood of my Lord and Savior Jesus Christ. I choose to be molded into Your image. I choose to walk in Your ways. I choose to be identified with You in Your death by taking up my cross daily, and in Your life by walking with You and choosing to serve my King, Jesus. I want to live pure, speak true, right wrong, and follow You, my King! By your grace and mercy and in Your name, I move forward as a new man in You. Amen."*

Listen to the Lord, so He can show You anything He needs to about your relationship with your dad. If there is anything you need to make right with dad, do it right away. This could also be a great time to just let your dad know how much you love and appreciate him.

Now, if you really prayed that prayer, your life can start changing right now. Find yourself in one of these three paragraphs:

If you already knew you were a Christian, have dealt with your past before, and dealt with any past issues and baggage with your dad, then this prayer was just a great reminder of your goals moving forward and a fresh start to where we're going in the book.

If you already knew you were a Christian, but have struggled with this very issue and the baggage it has created, then this could be a day of freedom for you. You have moved from the image of earthly dad into the image of your Heavenly Dad. But the good news is we're just getting started. We're going to look at building a life of purity, truth, and righteousness built on the fact that you are a beloved son and joint heir of the Most High God.

If you have never asked Christ into your life, but you sincerely prayed that prayer just now, I believe you are in, brother! That prayer also contained all the elements needed in asking for salvation and new life in Christ. The thief on the cross simply said. "Lord, will you remember me when you come into your kingdom?' Jesus responded (paraphrase): "Yes, in fact, you will be there with me today!" (Luke 23:42–43). I believe you just prayed a bit more than the thief on the cross.

You need to let someone know you have invited Jesus into your life. If you know a Christian brother, call him right now. If you don't know a brother, then call a Christian friend or family member to tell them. It doesn't matter what time it is, trust me, they will be thrilled you called. When they answer, just say, "Hey, I just prayed a prayer in this book and I asked Christ into my life." They will take it from there. If you don't know anyone to call, here's some action steps.

1.  Go to Page 233 in the back of this book.
2.  You need to find a local church and go tell the pastor about your decision. When you pray to receive Christ, you become a member of a family and the family needs to know you're in! That's what church is all about.

So, regardless of your past, I hope and pray we are all now in Christ as we move forward to see what His Spirit has for us, as we continue on in *The Knight's Code.*

*Jesus called them, and immediately they left the boat and their father and followed him.* —*Matthew 4:22* NIV

## DISCUSSION QUESTIONS

1.  Briefly share about your relationship with your dad—past and present.

2.  Discuss any parallel points in your relationship with your dad that Robert had with his.

3.  Why do you think we tend to either follow our father's pattern or we try to go the opposite direction?

4.  Why do you think our relationship with our dads affects our relationship with God so much?

5.  Discuss Luke 11:11–13 on Page 50.

6.  How has your relationship with your dad positively or negatively affected your image of God?

7.  Discuss any of your fears or dysfunctions that you blame on your dad today.

8.  What can you do to correct and change any negative and incorrect images that you have of God? Discuss.

9.  Under "Unpacking Baggage" on Page 56, give the number you feel that you are (10 percent–90 percent) and explain why.

10. Is there any authority that you still give your dad that really belongs to God? Discuss. (Reminder: This isn't removing a father's authority, but getting the authority and priority in the correct order as a man.)

Allow any men that are ready to pray the prayer on pages 57–58.

CHAPTER 5

# DISCOVERING YOUR LAWN LANGUAGE

*"When it comes to matters of the heart,*
*there ain't nothin' a fool won't get used to."* [1]
*—Michael McDonald*

Most of us are going to have to deal with taking care of a yard. If you live in a house, you probably have a yard. For many of us, this necessary evil will take up several weeks a year, throughout many years of our lives. Heck, you may be using this book as an excuse to put off mowing right now. (Glad I could help.)

My first yard was about half of the fifty-foot by one hundred-foot lot that my mobile home was parked on. I could mow it in about 20 minutes and, since I was single when I first lived there, I wasn't much into flowerbeds or shrubbery, so it was a fairly easy task. As a 20-year-old, I could get up on Saturday, mow, eat a bowl of cereal, and shower, all in under an hour. After I got married and began the typical upwardly mobile climb (pun intended) of the past 25 years, I now have about a third of an acre in a neighborhood where flowerbeds and shrubbery are an expectation. But the upside is my house no longer has wheels, so it can't be stolen in the middle of the night. But needless to say, the time, energy, and expense I go to are radically different from my mobile home days.

Regardless of where you live or your yard situation, if you're a guy, you're going to get this analogy.

## TURF TALK

Lawn care is now a $40 billion dollar industry in the U.S. That is about the size of the gross domestic product of the entire nation of Viet Nam.[2] (Can you say affluence?) A major focus of lawn care and the use of some of those billions have nothing to do with nurturing grass, but stopping and preventing the villain of the lawn world—the weed. Isn't it amazing how keeping your grass beautiful and green is an expensive and time-consuming job, yet growing giant, deep green weeds is so effortless and you can do it without spending a dime? They'll even spring up overnight through a crack in your sidewalk! Why can't golf course grass do that?!

So how can you have a lush, green yard? How can you end up with a beautiful bed of turf that golfers are tempted to practice putting on? You have to do two things. First, you must feed the grass the proper amount of water, nutrients, and fertilizer. Then, simultaneously you must get rid of weeds. For a pure lawn, you have to practice offense and defense. … *"Alright, lawn care and a sports metaphor! I'm with you now, Robert!"*

As I am writing this chapter, it is mid-March in Texas. My front yard is brown—all over. Zero green. It's not dead, just dormant. Contrast that to my neighbor that just had his yard mowed yesterday for the first time this season. I came home to see his freshly mowed and very green yard. Why did he already have to mow and why does his yard look so green? … weeds. That part of his yard is mostly weeds. Weeds that were already very visible and at least two inches tall, while my grass is still dormant. But in a few weeks, as my Bermuda Tiff 419 starts to wake up and grow, I'll be mowing too. Our neighbors will look over and see two very green yards. But one is green from grass and one is green from weeds. However, when they are freshly mowed, it is very difficult to see the difference.

But, in a few days, we will start to see the truth. Weeds start to grow quickly, get taller than the grass, and you clearly see them for what they are.

*"Okay, enough with the grass! What happened to sports? What's the point?"* … Well, here it is. Often, we as guys, will go to a men's conference, retreat, or other Christian event and hear some teaching, get convicted about something (or maybe a list of things), confess some sin, and commit to change and declare that we will start to lead and to give more and to serve more and … and … and, then by, oh say, the Wednesday after the event, life is back to normal. In fact, maybe even a step back from normal. Why? The sin that was confessed has returned with a vengeance and no real change stuck. But just days ago you felt on top of a mountain, ready to slay the dragons of your life and your family. But what did you really do? You went to an event, took a good look at your "weeds," and you "mowed" them, so they look good like the other guys' yards. By Wednesday, the weeds were still there, so they started growing and were quickly visible. And then you realized—"I didn't really rid myself of anything. Nothing really changed. I still have weeds."

Maybe this happens to you on a regular basis, maybe only occasionally. Some guys deal with this almost every Sunday. Many guys don't like feeling this way and church and Christian events just exacerbate the problem, so they just avoid going. It represents a standard we don't feel we can meet, or maybe just don't want to anymore, so we just quit. We get tired of mowing weeds, so we just give up. If you're a Christian guy and you rarely go to church anymore, I'll bet this has something to do with your absence. Often, it's not really that you don't love God, it's that you're sick of being sick and being reminded you're sick. You decided to just let the weeds take over. It's just not worth the time and effort anymore—so you think.

> IT'S NOT REALLY THAT YOU DON'T LOVE GOD, IT'S THAT YOU'RE SICK OF BEING SICK AND BEING REMINDED YOU'RE SICK.

Some men don't actually give up, but they just decide to mask the truth and look good at all costs. They will even teach a Sunday school class or take some other leadership role, so they can tell someone else what needs to be changed and they can then avoid their own conviction. Just keep the weeds mowed and coast until Heaven. Many churches don't mind guys doing this, because it fills desperately needed ministry positions. And after all, we can sacrifice a brother to get a ministry slot filled, can't we? You know, take one for the team.

If you're one of those guys that looking good at all costs is really important—to keep a yard full of weeds looking decent, you have to mow a lot more. You have to work hard to not let anyone know you haven't taken care of your yard, to keep up the appearance, so no one finds out you have weeds. God forbid our Christian brothers see we have weeds in our yard! To look like the nice lawn guy, you have to work twice as hard, mow twice as much.

Regardless of how good or horrible the "yard of your heart" looks, you're about to get an opportunity to get serious about your issues. Whether you look at your yard and see a handful of weeds or you are overwhelmed because you can't even see grass anymore, please know that purity, truth, and righteousness can be yours. Christ offers these virtues to ANY man who will follow Him. Remember this from Chapter 2: *One of the major premises of the Knight's Code is any type, size, age, or make of man can develop these qualities in his life. No man has an edge over another man. It's not about the body, but the heart. It's not about the strength of the arm, but the strength of the soul.*

The cycle can end. A new life can begin. No matter how many weeds you have, your yard can be way more pure than it is now, than it has ever been. We won't ever be perfect (sin-less) this side of Heaven, but one of the obedience points of the Christian faith is to "pull weeds" when we see them. When Jesus points to a weed, we must take action. *"If your right eye causes you to sin, gouge it out ... "* That's the idea (Matthew 5:29 NIV).

## BURN BAN

Growing up in the '60s in north central Texas, long before builders started sodding yards, homeowners just let the grass that was there from the original cow pasture grow back up. (Pretty much all the land in Texas was a cow pasture at one time.) As a result, a major problem we had was "grass burrs." Now, if you don't know what that is, it is the biggest, baddest weed ever! First, it shoots up a tall, dark green stalk, and then begins to produce these round spheres covered in sharp spikes. (I believe these may be classified as medieval weapons.) One grass burr can produce as many as 25 spiked balls. These things are lethal and if you ever fell down in a patch of them, well, they can make a grown man cry, because they stick deep and they hurt for a long time after you pull them out.

When I was a kid, our yard was covered with grass burrs. Falling down in our yard was suicide, or murder, depending on if you got pushed. My dad tried everything to get rid of our grass burrs and chemicals like *Round Up* hadn't been invented yet.

My dad was a smoker, so I think he always viewed fire as his ally. One early summer evening, he had had it with the grass burrs! In the words of Popeye, "It was all he could stands, he couldn't stands no more!" So my dad hooked up the water hose in the front yard, took out his matches, and effectively set the entire front yard on fire. He started his own grass fire. … well, grass burr fire. He went over and wet down our neighbor's yard and sprayed water on our frame house (yes, made completely of wood). Thank God he was able to contain the fire and caused no major damage. At the end of this adventure, our yard was a smoldering, black mess. As a kid, I think I was somewhere in between shock and "ah, cool!" My mom just stayed in the house, curtains drawn.

Now, here's the crazy thing (like the fire wasn't?). Within about two weeks, the yard began to turn green and life re-emerged from the ashes, but … so did the grass burrs. In fact, they came back with a vengeance. Why? The plants were burned *on top* of the ground, but the roots were still very much alive *in* the ground. My dad took care of the seen, but not the unseen. The real culprit went untouched—the root. The only way to effectively remove a grass burr plant is to pull it out by the roots and that takes a ton of work, time, and energy. (Then you can burn 'em.)

A lot of guys take a look at their lives—like my dad looked at his yard—and realize they don't like what it has become and it's going to take a lot of work to change. Then there are thoughts like: "What I intended to become is not what I am." "Life hasn't turned out at all like I thought it would." "This is not how I saw my future when I was younger." So, they throw up their hands and light a match to their lives. They think, "What the Hell, just burn it up! It's gone anyway."

THE FIRE THEY START IS A VISIBLE SYMPTOM THAT HIDES A DEEP INVISIBLE NEED.

The fire may be an affair, debt, porn, gambling, drinking, drugs, whatever. The fire they start is a visible symptom that hides a deep invisible need.

Guys, let's commit right now to put away the matches and to stop mowing weeds. Haven't we had enough of the vicious cycle? We're going to have to get down on our knees and do some pulling, right out by the roots. It's dirty. It's hard work and you end up with holes in your yard, dirt exposed, where the root was. It doesn't look real pretty at first when you pull a bunch of weeds. But, oh man, next spring, you are going to be so glad you did work on your yard.

## YOUR ONE THING

I need to warn you that once you start this process, it never ends. Our sin will always produce weeds, so to maintain purity, you must keep pulling. We have to identify, through the Holy Spirit, the weeds/sins we have and begin to pull them out one at a time. Some are gone forever, some return next week. But the Lord will give us the strength and grace to deal with it. He knows exactly what to do and when.

The late and great communicator/author Dave Busby used to often say when he spoke, "Now that my talk is done, if you feel like you have a list of things you have to go home and work on, then just know that you got your list from Satan, because he wants to overwhelm you, cause you to quit trying to rid yourself of sin, and give up. If, however, you hear a still, small voice whispering one thing you need to work on, you can trust that is the voice of Jesus. He gives you one thing at a time to work on. Now go home and work on your one thing."

If you feel overwhelmed at your weeds and don't know where to begin, try this. Speaking out loud, confess everything you can think of that needs to be confessed. Throw up all your sin and then listen to Him tell you how and where to start pulling. He will. As Dave Busby said, Jesus will take one issue at a time and deal with you, showing you how to rid yourself of each one. As my friend and counselor Dr. Ed Laymance says, "You peel an onion one layer at a time." Some issues will be easy and may only take days, while some will be very tough and take many years. The important thing is to keep giving it all to Christ and not give up. Keep pulling. Keep peeling. By His strength. Through His grace.

*"So we're not giving up. How could we! Even though on the outside it often looks like things are falling apart on us, on the inside, where God is making new life, not a day goes by without his unfolding grace. These hard times are small potatoes compared to the coming good times, the lavish celebration prepared for us. There's far more here than meets the eye. The things we see now are here today, gone tomorrow. But the things we can't see now will last forever." —2 Corinthians 4:16–18* MSG

We have laid a lot of groundwork (another pun intended). Now let's move into the *Live Pure* chapters. Roll up your sleeves, guys. Real change is never easy, but when it comes from Jesus, it's always good.

## DISCUSSION QUESTIONS

1.  Discuss lawn care for a few minutes. Is it a necessary evil for you or a habitual hobby? Why is it a $40 billion dollar industry in this nation?

2.  Why is "weeds in the yard" a good analogy to the sin in our hearts? Or is it? Discuss.

3.  Have you ever had a mountaintop spiritual experience and then wondered where it went in just a few days? Discuss.

4.  Why do you think some men just quit caring about change and give up?

5.  Why do you think some men focus only on making sure they look good or that everything appears to be right, even though it's really not?

6.  Why do we fight the process of "pulling weeds" from our lives? What makes it so hard? Why is it easier to take care of the "seen" and not the "unseen?"

7.  Read and discuss the bold insert statement on Page 66. What are some fires that you are tempted with right now?

8.  Is confession of sin to God easy or difficult for you? Discuss.

9.  Is confession to a brother easy or difficult for you? Discuss.

10. Do you know your "one thing" today? Take the rest of the time to share and pray each man's "one thing." If a man isn't ready to share, then simply pray for him.

CHAPTER 6

# *LIVE PURE*
# GOD OWNS THE WHOLE WORKS

*"That's just the way it is.*
*Some things will never change.*
*That's just the way it is.*
*Oh, but don't you believe them."* [1]
—Bruce Hornsby

There's an old joke that goes … A guy was in his psychiatrist's office and the doctor decides to take him through Rorschach's inkblot test to get into the depths of his psyche. He holds up the first inkblot and asks, "What do you see when you look at this?" The guy stares at it for a moment and confidently answers, "sex." The doctor is a bit surprised, but moves on to the next blot. "Okay, tell me what you see when you look at this one?" The guy sighs deeply, pauses, and again says, "Well … sex." Puzzled, the psychiatrist goes through several more and every time the patient, by now blushing and embarrassed, answers hesitantly with "sex." The doctor finally slams down the inkblots and yells, "You are sick, man! How can you see sex in every one of these?!" The man, now frustrated too, yells back, "Me?! You're the one with all the dirty pictures!!"

As guys, we relate a lot of things to sex, whether it appears to be related to sex or not! The craziest things can trigger a sexual thought. Because of these mental connections, the word "purity" usually relates primarily to one thing for us—sex. Interesting how such an innocent concept can produce very impure connotations.

## It's a Soul Thing

We've learned through society, as well as in our Christian paradigm, that purity applies primarily to our sexual being. But the problem is that's not Biblical.

*"The physical part of you is not some piece of property belonging to the spiritual part of you. God owns the whole works.—1 Corinthians 6:20 MSG*

True Biblical purity is so much deeper and broader than just sex. It's about your inner life, your thought life, the deep recesses of your heart. Sex is definitely a *part* of that, but not *all* of that. We're talking about a purity that really isn't just a body thing, or even a mind thing, but a soul thing. Now, the issue is what comes out of the soul, then goes through the mind, and out through the body. Our actions are born from thoughts rooted in our souls. And much of those thoughts are born out of what we perceive our needs to be. Much of our sin is rooted in us wanting those needs met. And sin would like them met when? Right now!

> TRUE BIBLICAL PURITY IS SO MUCH DEEPER AND BROADER THAN JUST SEX.

*"You have heard that it was said, 'Do not commit adultery.' But I tell you that anyone who looks at a woman lustfully has already committed adultery with her in his heart." —Jesus in Matthew 5:27–28 NIV*

No matter how well you believe you know this Scripture, reason with me for a moment. When Jesus made this statement, everyone knew the Law said that adultery was forbidden. The connotation applied to this word in Jesus' day was solely connected to the physical act of sex with someone other than your spouse. But watch this …

In this statement, Jesus, from that day forward, effectively and completely:

~ *redefined* adultery.

No longer was it just about the physical act. The physical act is simply the completion of, or the acting out of, the thought that motivates the sin. Jesus now says the sin has already been committed when the thought occurs—and entertained in the mind.

~ *defined* the spirit behind the Law.

God always has a life principle behind every commandment or law. It's not so much about the "what" as the "why." To God, the "why" creates the "what." The spirit of the Law is not so much about adultery, as it is about being pure in your soul. The Law says don't commit adultery. The spirit of the law is do not think about another woman as you would your own wife. See the bigger picture? To be pure, to be holy as He is holy, do not think about another woman in this manner. And the practical side is if it is stopped in the mind, the action will never be carried out.

~ *refined* the definition of purity.

True purity is the absence of the motive or thought that would motivate the wrong action. And this is the ultimate goal for us in every aspect of our life, not just sexual. Remove the motive, which then kills the thought, which then stops the action—before it takes place.

So, suddenly you have a group of men listening to Jesus who believe they are not guilty of ever committing adultery (and darn proud of it, I might add), who are now having to count up the number of times they have sinned and they are running out of fingers. ... Definitely an "oh crap!" moment for them. ... *"Surely He doesn't mean even if you just think about it?! Do you think He really means that? ... Do we really have to gouge out our eyes?! I mean, hypothetically of course, if we ever really did think about another woman?"*

Jesus effectively forever changed the purity paradigm for men in one simple statement. (He had a tendency to do that kind of thing, didn't He?) This now calls for an entirely different method of maintaining purity. Now, it is not enough to keep myself out of the wrong bed, but to keep myself out of a wrong state of mind. A little trickier, huh? I must keep my soul on track, not simply my physical being.

Let's say you and a couple of guys meet regularly for accountability and prayer. For most Christian guys, it is going to be fairly easy to make sure you all stay out of a situation to have sex with someone other than your spouse. You can tell each other where you were physically this past week. You can report to each other your whereabouts on business trips. You can account for your physical life. You have a good shot at being successful at avoiding adultery by simply knowing you will have to report to your brothers.

But, does it not change everything to agree that our goal is to get to the place where we are not even going to *think* about it?! Suddenly, it's not so much about my calendar anymore, or simply staying away from certain situations, or certain women. It's no longer enough to just divulge my whereabouts and actions, so you know I didn't get into trouble. To maintain purity, I now have to talk to you about my thoughts, desires, and motives. Purity now begins where it has always begun—at its source—my soul and mind. Jesus knew that then. Jesus knows that now. He was and is a Master at cutting through the symptoms and getting to the real root of the problem. When You're the Creator of all things, You can do that really well.

When the Law states "do not commit adultery," that only attacks the symptom, not the root. Jesus showed us the root. Ironic that one of His names is *The Root of Jesse.* I understand that name has to do with genealogy and prophecy, but He continually, in situation after situation in Scripture, shows us the root of the problem with our sin.

## TRIED TO MAKE ME GO TO REHAB, BUT I SAID NO, NO, NO

For many years, our culture has treated symptoms, not the root cause. What is always the answer when a celebrity gets into trouble? … One word—rehab. Rehab is the magic bullet. It's the Golden Ticket for the return to celebrity-dom. *"I had two affairs, had an illegitimate child, and burned down an old folks home. But! It's ok 'cause I spent three weeks and $150,000 in rehab."* To which we humbly respond, *"Thanks so much for coming clean and for your sacrifice to humanity. You may now once again grace the cover of People Magazine and be on Oprah."*

Name any celebrity that has been caught in a major issue in the past five years and what did you always hear at some point? A trip to rehab. Go get rid of the symptoms. A guy admits a sin or confesses an addiction and we work on helping him stop the actions. But that rarely works. … Why? Because stopping the actions doesn't change the heart. Yes, we must stop the actions; but that doesn't uncover the unmet need that drove him to self-destruction to begin with. By the time I have acted out on a thought, it is in its end form. The issue began in my heart and soul, then seeped into my mind, and eventually into my body and out through my actions. Then I begin training myself to repeat the pattern.

To be clear—rehab, therapy, counseling, and support groups are great! I recommend professional help. My life has been saved and much improved by Biblical counseling on many occasions. But that is a start, not the end. So many folks end up back at square one, because the root of the problem isn't found.

Several years ago, I saw a man interviewed on *Good Morning America* that had been caught in incest with his teenage daughter. He had gone through extensive counseling and therapy, he and his wife had gone through counseling together, and the family had been in counseling. He was now "speaking out" about the hidden issue of incest to try and shed light on this taboo topic to save other families from the horrors of this sin of secrecy. At the end of the interview, the host asked him, "So, after all these many hours of counseling and therapy, the question I most want to ask is this: Why? … Did you uncover why you would do this to your own daughter?" The man paused and calmly answered, "No, we could never figure that out." The interview ended. Cut to commercial.

Here's my bet: if that guy stopped his sexual acting out with his daughter, but didn't figure out the "why" in his own soul, he will act out in some other way in the not too distant future. We would all agree that stopping incest will always be the right thing to do, but while they may have successfully ended one problem, they left a time bomb ticking with a thousand other ways to act out. If we are addicts, we can find something to get addicted to.

Again I will repeat, the only way any man is going to get to the root of his issues to find real answers for his soul is through a relationship with Jesus Christ.

*"Thomas said to him, "Lord, we don't know where you are going, so how can we know the way?" Jesus answered, "I am the way and the truth and the life. No one comes to the Father except through me." —John 14:5–6 NIV*

## THROWING UP THE SYMPTOMS

In my ministry to men over the years, here's a typical scenario. A guy calls and nervously asks to meet with me. He comes in and I say, "Alright, tell me what's going on." He stutters and him-haws and shuffles and apologizes and all the nervous guy stuff that we all do. He says he's going to tell me something he's never told anyone, that he is so ashamed, and that he is likely about to destroy my entire view of him in a single sentence. Sometimes there's sweating, sometimes crying. Finally, like a man with a horribly nauseated stomach, he throws up something like, "I'm an alcoholic." Or "I have a porn problem." Or "I have a gambling addiction." Or "I struggle with homosexuality." Or "I had an affair." You name it. I've heard it. The symptoms are endless, but the root cause is always the same—a heart problem. And that's true for each of us and for all of our sin.

My response to these men has always been the same. "Okay, now that we've gotten the symptom out that's been eating at you, please know I don't condemn you. Please know this is a place of grace and that I am totally fine with you. Your sin is no more hideous to God than mine. In fact, I respect the fact that you would confess and desire to change. Now, that the confession is out of the way, let's talk about why this has happened or is happening and where it came from. Let's get to the root of this issue."

Do you see it? It's not really about what they came in to confess. For the guy, that's the hard part. For me, that's the easy part. It's figuring out the "why" now that the "what" is exposed. That's the tough job! If a guy doesn't figure out what's behind the "why," he will likely just find a new "what" or just keep struggling with the old one.

I have found that 99.9 percent of Christian guys that will walk in and confess a sin have already beaten themselves up so badly on an emotional and spiritual level that if it showed on them physically, they would be unrecognizable as a human. There is zero sense in one brother spiritually "beating up" another brother with a condemnation stick, especially when he is coming to obey Scripture and confess sin to a brother for help and restoration. In Christ, there is no condemnation (Romans 8:1). There are consequences, but not condemnation.

Gentlemen, I'm not speaking this *from* a pastoral responsibility, but rather, from brother *to* brother. We all have to learn this, so we can really help each other become godly men. We must speak truth to each other. We must help each other deal with the consequences. But we must provide grace for each other to do the right thing with the sin, so we can get better, so we can move on in health, so we can live pure to further God's Kingdom. There aren't enough pastors or shrinks in the world to get to us all. That's why a major push of this book is for us to help each other. You know, actually be the church! Act like brothers! Be there for each other.

When was the last time you hung your head before Jesus to confess a sin and suddenly you found yourself in the middle of a Messianic brow beating? Doesn't happen. When was the last time you confessed and heard His Spirit say anything other than, "You're forgiven. Now, go and sin no more." The brow beating comes from two sources: our own minds and the enemy. Okay, maybe in your life, it's three. Maybe the church you go to helps. One of the many reasons confession is lost to this generation in the church is the fear of rejection and condemnation. Here's the difference: Jesus disciplines, He doesn't destroy. As brothers and as the church, we too must practice discipline, but not destroy. Get the symptom confessed, so we can get to the real problem. Confession is not an end, but simply a beginning to the process of restoration. Throwing up the symptoms is the start to finding answers. Receiving and responding to discipline helps get us back in line with God and each other.

> CONFESSION IS NOT AN END, BUT SIMPLY A BEGINNING TO THE PROCESS OF RESTORATION. THROWING UP THE SYMPTOMS IS THE START TO FINDING ANSWERS.

## TIME TO CHANGE YOUR MIND?

Taking in all that we have discussed thus far in this chapter, please allow me to ask: What is the only Entity that could possibly saturate our souls to the point of providing protection from our very own minds? The only One I personally know of is the Holy Spirit of God.

*But the Counselor, the Holy Spirit, whom the Father will send in my name, will teach you all things and will remind you of everything I have said to you. —John 14:26 NIV*

Who else can dive down into our motives and purify the very fiber of where our decisions are born? Who else can right our wrongs? I have personally found on countless occasions that I cannot do this myself. I have tried a thousand times and I have failed a thousand times. But Jesus said that His Spirit will teach us all things and remind us of what we need to know.

Let me be boldly honest with you. One of the greatest contradictions in life is someone who believes he has secured a home in Heaven, but lives helpless in Hell right here. Regardless of whether or not you are a Christian or where you stand spiritually right now, regardless of how filthy you may feel or what you are guilty of, regardless of how shameful you are of your private thoughts, God provides a path to purity. He can replace your shame with His grace. He can heal you, deliver you, and rescue you. That's His specialty. No one else can accomplish those things. He does it every day for those who call on His name. How do I know? How can I say that with such certainty? Because He has done it for me and continues to on a daily basis. Once His healing begins, it continues on for life. Remember what I said in chapter one: I'm not writing this book from being some kind of expert, but only out of personal experience. The only thing I am an expert on is that I know you and I need Christ!

If you dreaded reading these *Live Pure* chapters because you are sick of the conviction and condemnation regarding your purity, if you avoid church or Christian men's meetings because you don't want to hear one more time what you're *not* doing, then hopefully you've heard some good news in these pages.

*Live Pure* is not about reminding us all of how desperately sick we are. Most of us get that already. It is to focus on the fact that there are real answers for our souls. Mine and yours. If you are defeated by the way you have learned to live in your soul, Jesus can begin to change your mind—quite literally. So, hang on and read on. Lift your head and look for Him in the words written here. This chapter has laid the foundation for where we're going in regards to purity.

## DISCUSSION QUESTIONS

1.  Read and discuss the bold insert statement on Page 70. Why do you think we associate our purity primarily on sexual issues?

2.  Read Matthew 5:27–28 on Page 70. Discuss why you think Jesus redefined and refined the idea of adultery.

3.  Why is it important to find the root of our problems and not just treat the symptoms?

4.  Have you ever struggled with why you keep doing something, even though you hate it every time you do it? Why do we do this?

5.  Do you struggle with "beating yourself up" when you blow it?

6.  Why do you think we as men get so tired of hearing about our problems, but yet we struggle to be pro-active to apply the answers we do find?

7.  How can we start helping each other figure out the "why" and not just the "what" of our issues? Discuss practical solutions.

8.  Discuss the importance of maintaining a non-condemning place for guys to share their stuff. How do we do this? How do we make sure we act like brothers and not judges?

9.  How can we as brothers provide discipline for each other? Discuss practical ways to do this.

10. Do you really believe God has a path to purity for you? Do you really believe you can accept that and begin to walk there with Him?

    Close in prayer.

CHAPTER 7

# *LIVE PURE*
## SUPPLY & DEMAND

*"Well, I'm watching the dragons as they make another claim.*
*He used to be a friend of mine. I called him by name.*
*And I'm watching the dragons as they slither out of sight, tonight."* [1]
—*Edwin McCain*

As we have stated, most men think of their lust problem as a sexual issue. The first thing to understand is that it is NOT a sexual issue. Lust is a heart problem. Lust is a symptom, not the root cause. The root is disobedience. The root is trying to meet a need in our own way, rather than giving it to God and allowing Him to meet the need in His way. If you see lust as the only issue, then you work to not lust, but then here comes the lust anyway. Why? You aren't addressing the real problem.

## NON-FICTION & FANTASY

I have two close friends that have nearly identical stories. Both are now in their thirties, both professionals, one married, one divorced, both with children. Everything I could write about one is true of the other. But they are not alone. Their story is in process all over this nation in hundreds of thousands of men, all in different places along this path. See if you are in their story, and if so, where you are in it.

Both these guys were raised in Christian homes. Different levels of commitment, but both church-going, solid families. Years ago in high school and college, they discovered pornography. The printed kind. The pictures in magazines. The ones that were hidden under the bed.

Of course, pornography isn't the end; it's the means. The end goal is meeting an emotional need and sexual desire. Porn is the stimulus to get the need met. For these guys, the cycle continued in secret for many years.

Both led very normal, productive lives, dating in high school and college and working hard at their jobs. Both very nice guys who would give you the shirt off their back. They each eventually met the woman of their dreams and married. They made the same promises we all make at the altar. But back in the secret room of their hearts, a wildfire was blazing out of control.

Next, enter the age of the Internet and both soon discovered online porn. The quick accessibility in so many places poured fuel on the fire and the problem became an addiction. Now both had an ever-growing "weed" that was slowly taking over the "yard." Every failure, every stress, and even every victory led back to the same thing—porn. It became the end result of just about everything and consumed more and more time, which caused the need to lie, and to hide more. The isolation drove them both deeper into the problem. The vicious cycle finally went into full destruction mode.

As with any lust and addiction, regardless of its object, the need gets increasingly difficult to satisfy, so it demands and requires more and more. (One of the many reasons why there is a new Playmate every month and the porn industry has to keep finding fresh meat.) Finally, it is no longer enough to simply look at digital images and fantasize. The desire leads to wanting to act these visualizations out with someone. And it's not that the woman has to look like the Photoshopped and airbrushed girls do in the photos, as long as they will do the things the ones in the photos will do or imagine them to do. (This is why almost every time you see a guy's "mistress," she is usually not as attractive as the guy's spouse. Tiger Woods and Jesse James are classic examples.)

One of my friends found his "mistress" through a chat room and discovered she was local. The chats turned into phone calls, the phone calls to meetings, the meetings to sexual liasons. The other friend found his "mistress" through a "just dropped by to see how you were doing" from a woman met through his business. Enough signals and the right language revealed she was interested. The rest of both stories are the same.

As with most all on-going affairs, the truth eventually came out, the spouse found out, and it became "public." At this point with both friends, I was the first person they called. And I had no idea it was going on, either time.

I'll stop here with their stories, because what happened from there for both of them isn't relevant to the subject matter of these chapters. Plus I need to get to the point for you and this is the best place to do that.

Is there any part of their story where you saw yourself? Could, at any point, one of them just as easily be you? Did you recognize your own journey as we went down their paths?

Maybe this is your story too and you are down the road and re-covering, or maybe your life was destroyed at the point I stopped the story and you are trying to rebuild. If so, I'm really glad you are reading this book, because I pray it can help you on your road to healing. But my first objective at this moment is if you see your own life inside one of the stages of their story—right now.

Here's a very common thing for us guys to think, and both my friends did it too. At whatever point you are now, you swear you won't take it any farther. "Yeah, I spend several hours a week on-line, but I can quit when I want to." "Well, I may be struggling with porn, but I would never have an affair!" "Okay, I've been flirting with this girl and it's getting pretty dirty, but I would never actually do anything."

"Okay, so I slept with her once. I won't see her again. I'm done with it." … Are any of these you? Have you—do you—think these things?

Guys, if this is not you, if you have not struggled in this area, that is awesome, but I am begging you to keep reading because you have friends right now, just like I did, that are trapped in this private Hell and they need you to crawl into the fire and pull them out! If you have a circle of guys that you are buds with, I guarantee you that at least one of them is at some point in this story. … *"So, Robert, how can I know with my friends? How can I find out when it's kept such a deep secret?"* … Great question. Here's what you can do. Get your friends together in a circle and simply tell them that if any of them are struggling with a sin, addiction, or issue, and they feel trapped, that you want to help. You want to help them before it is too late. Be very direct and make yourself available. Tell them that if they can't bring themselves to talk about it now, that you are ready 24/7 to help. Then tell them that you want to stay pure in your life and you need prayer and help to continue on your path. None of us are experts, just fellow strugglers. (Do you see how this ties back to what we discussed in Chapter 3?)

Now, back to you guys who are in your own version of my friends' stories. What should you do? First, you are going to have to be honest with yourself. You could slip farther down and go to the next step and it could happen at any time. You could fall deeper. You are going to have to realize you are not the exception to the rule. Listen, if either of my friends could talk to you knee-to-knee right now, they would plead with you to stop and get help. They've been exactly where you are. They wish to God every day that they had taken steps before it went where it did for them. They wish they had listened to all the times their God whispered in their ear to turn away from the addiction and turn to Him. … Now, it's your turn.

Maybe you need to put this book down right now and grab your phone and call a brother. Call your pastor. Maybe you need to get in your car and drive to a friend's house right now and look him in the eye and get help. (I once had a guy call me at 1:30 in the morning to tell me he was on his way to my house.) If you sense a conviction in your spirit to do something right now and you don't act on it, then every time you say no to that voice, you sear your conscience and callous up a little more to God, until one day you won't give a rip what anyone says, including Him. Seen it happen too many times. So, … PUT THE BOOK DOWN AND MAKE A PHONE CALL OR START DRIVING TO THE FRIEND'S HOUSE. ACT. MOVE. TAKE CHARGE. LISTEN TO THE SPIRIT OF GOD CALLING YOU HOME. DO NOT WAIT. YOU ARE WORTH IT. YOUR FAMILY IS WORTH IT. YOUR FAITH IS WORTH IT. YOU CAN END THIS RIGHT HERE, RIGHT NOW!

If this is not your issue or problem, and you are ready to move forward with the next step of this chapter, I want to ask you to do something a little strange, especially coming from a book. Would you stop right now and pray for your brothers out there reading this book that need to take action to end their sin and addiction? What if right now there's a guy in another city reading this too and your prayer could make the difference in him getting help? Would you pray for the guys who will read this book in the future? Maybe you know a friend who has this book lying in his house? Pray that God's Spirit would use these words to move men to action in the area of purity. Pray that men would end their walk down this path to destruction, get help, get accountability, and start "pulling weeds," allowing Jesus to minister His grace and redemption to their hearts and rebuild their lives in Him. Can you imagine if every guy that reads this chapter would either pray for God to move in the hearts of his unseen brothers out there OR take action to stop their own path toward destruction? … Yeah, that would be cool alright. My two friends would sure think so. And they know exactly what to pray right now.

## SOMEONE, SOMEWHERE CARES FOR HER SOUL

Christian author, communicator, and radio host Dawson McAllister defines lust as "caring more for a woman's body than her soul." Try this. Picture Jesus as Mary Magdalene is walking up to Him. Can you imagine Him eyeing her up and down? Looking at her hind-end and breasts? … No. He looked her in the eyes and cared about her soul EVERY time she walked up to Him. Because of this, she felt safe and didn't feel threatened like she did from pretty much every other man in her life in that day. That's why Mary liked hanging out with Jesus. He was different. He lived pure. And she was safe.

Now especially if you've been a Christian for a long time, you probably read my Jesus/Mary Magdalene analogy and cringed, right? You thought, *"Man, I can't believe you said that!"* Well, as a Christian, we need to get to the point where we cringe about it for ourselves, not just thinking about if Jesus had done it!

I'm not saying any of us are going to hit perfection this side of Heaven, but is Jesus' life not the example and goal for us as Christian men? What's your current goal for purity? Think about the women in your life that you truly care for their souls. Your mom? Your wife? Daughter? Daughter-in-law? If you're married, do you want your best buds to care about your wife's body or her soul? If you have a teenage daughter, do you want your best buds to care about her body or her soul?

Do you see how if you truly began to care for ALL women's souls like you do for these women, that you don't have to focus so much on not lusting? You begin to focus on *doing the right thing,* rather than *not doing the wrong thing.* It's a perspective change. It's now more about offense and not so much about defense. Aren't you ready to not be on the defense so much in this area?

> YOU BEGIN TO FOCUS ON *DOING THE RIGHT THING,* RATHER THAN *NOT DOING THE WRONG THING.* IT'S A PERSPECTIVE CHANGE.

The hooker on the street has someone, somewhere that cares for her soul. It may only be a grandmother she hasn't seen in years. The Playmate has someone, somewhere that cares for her soul. It may only be the little boy she is raising alone, who is the only reason she posed to begin with because she needed the money. But that detail is not in her bio, because it's not "hot." Well, we need to be Jesus men who care for these women's souls. And the girl at your office. The woman who lives down the street. The waitress. The secretary. Care for their soul. Jesus did. Jesus does. We can too. After all, we represent Him as His ambassadors. It's a paradigm shift. The knight's chivalry was born out of this attitude. Saving, not savaging. Respecting, not ravaging. Caring for the soul of a woman.

## But With God ...

The enemy has done a good job of spreading a lie over generations. He tells men every day that—Jesus or no Jesus—no man can live without lust. If he can convince you that you have no choice; in fact, if you're a red-blooded man, you *should* lust, then he has a greater shot at robbing and destroying you (John 10:10). It doesn't matter if you are a teenager, a single man in his 20's, or a middle-ager that has been married for 20 years, lust can be dealt with. I am not saying it will never be a temptation. Let me repeat that. I am not saying it will never be a temptation. But lust can be brought under the submission of Christ. Through Him, it can be controlled and it can be stopped. Jesus proved that. He proved that a man can live his life, control Himself, and care about women's souls. He is our Example and our Goal.

My personal—not theological—opinion is that one of the many reasons that Jesus never married was to show us the level of self-control and obedience that is available through a life surrendered to God's power. That same power can end the lust problem in your life. Temptation will still come, but you can deal with it the way He did by giving it to God. Surrender. I really don't believe a man can put a stop to the demon of lust without the power of Christ, but I also don't believe a man can have any lasting change of *any* kind outside of the power of Christ. (Recurring theme!)

If there is anything in our lives that you and I decide cannot be defeated, then that means there is something that God cannot do, and then that means that He is not God. And that is not true. I have been walking with Him for decades now and I have seen that He can stop anything. He can change anything, but it has to be given to Him first. Surrender.

He said it Himself in Matthew 19:26 (NIV): *With man this is impossible, but with God all things are possible.*

Let's insert our new paradigm: *With man [defeating lust and impurity] is impossible, but with God [being pure] is possible.*

If you go through the Gospels and only read where Jesus dealt with women, first of all, you will notice He connected with a good amount of females. Mary and Martha were some of his closest friends. Second, you will see that the conversation was always about either the woman or His Father. He didn't talk about Himself, unless it was to make a reference about God. (What do you tend to talk about with women?)

And do you think there was a remote possibility that Mary Magdalene was attractive? Or how about the woman at the well who had been with a number of men? I doubt all these women in these situations were ugly. Jesus had to look into the eyes of very attractive women and care for their souls. We can too. Why? Because of Him. Period.

> JESUS HAD TO LOOK INTO THE EYES OF VERY ATTRACTIVE WOMEN AND CARE FOR THEIR SOULS. WE CAN TOO.

Let me stop and ask you a really serious question: Do women feel comfortable around you or do you make them feel like they need to go through a purification rite after they've walked away? The ladies you work with? The waitresses at your favorite restaurants? Women at your work-out facility? The ladies who frequent your Starbucks? And even the women you know at church? Especially anywhere you frequent and see the same women over and over again? If they all got together and discussed you, what would they say regarding you? Would they talk about how you check them out? Talk about how you look them up and down? Comment on how you probably couldn't tell the color of their eyes, because you never look them in the eye? Maybe you've gone way past that and they would talk about how flirty you are and the suggestive comments you make?

Or would they comment on what a gentleman you are and how you look them in the eyes when you speak to them? Would they say you are a man of honor? Would they talk about how much you respect women and how blessed your wife must be to have such a great guy? Would they connect the word "chivalry" to you?

Which guy are you? Which guy do you want to be? Well, one of those guys you can be on your own. The other guy requires Christ to become. Every day.

A primary difference in the two situations I've presented here is one guy makes it about him and the other guy makes it about her. You see that? Women can spot that a mile away. Women know when a man is respecting them. Women are onto guys way more than we think. And the ladies that are naïve and don't get it? Unfortunately they usually end up hurt … by guys.

Allow me to close this chapter by addressing a thought I hear occasionally. Some guys think if the girls that pose for the porn pictures would just stop, then they wouldn't be tempted to look. To put this in business terms, that is focusing on supply. Now let's turn that around. What if the demand for these "models" ended? You think when the money dried up that these women would keep taking their clothes off? Do we really think they're doing it for the reasons that get fantasized about? We know better than that. The porn industry is not about sex—it's about money. Just like with prostitution, when the money ain't there, the clothes stay on. Porn will go away when the demand stops. Living pure is choking the demand out of our lives. One guy at a time. One soul at a time.

Take in David's words, written after his sin with Bathsheba, his responsibility for the death of her husband, and the birth of a child fathered in adultery. In these words are the hope for every man.

*Generous in love—God, give grace!*
*Huge in mercy—wipe out my bad record.*
*Scrub away my guilt, soak out my sins in your laundry.*
*I know how bad I've been; my sins are staring me down.*
*You're the One I've violated, and you've seen*
*it all, seen the full extent of my evil.*
*You have all the facts before you;*
*whatever you decide about me is fair.*
*I've been out of step with you for a long time,*
*in the wrong since before I was born.*
*What you're after is truth from the inside out.*
*Enter me, then; conceive a new, true life.*
*Soak me in your laundry and I'll come out clean,*
*scrub me and I'll have a snow-white life.*
*Tune me in to foot-tapping songs,*
*set these once-broken bones to dancing.*
*Don't look too close for blemishes, give me a clean bill of health.*
*God, make a fresh start in me,*
*shape a Genesis week from the chaos of my life.*
*Don't throw me out with the trash, or fail to breathe holiness in me.*
*Bring me back from gray exile, put a fresh wind in my sails!*
*Give me a job teaching rebels your ways*
*so the lost can find their way home.*
*Commute my death sentence, God, my salvation God,*
*and I'll sing anthems to your life-giving ways.*
*Unbutton my lips, dear God; I'll let loose with your praise.*
*Going through the motions doesn't please you,*
*a flawless performance is nothing to you.*
*I learned God-worship when my pride was shattered.*
*Heart-shattered lives ready for love*
*don't for a moment escape God's notice.*
*—Psalm 51:1–17 MSG*

## DISCUSSION QUESTIONS

1.  Discuss the opening statements of the chapter on Page 79: "Lust is not a sexual issue. Lust is a heart problem. Lust is a symptom, not the root cause." Agree/disagree? Why?

2.  Why do you think Robert's story of his two friends is such a common occurrence these days?

3.  Why do you think addiction to pornography is so rampant?

4.  Why do you think pornography today can feel so private and anonymous?

5.  Why do we as men always want to believe we have life under control?

6.  Why are sexual temptations and struggles such a difficult topic for us as guys to talk openly about?

7.  Discuss the phrase at the top of page 84, "Lust is caring more for a woman's body than you do her soul."

8.  Discuss how you deal with the women in your life. Talk about the ladies at your work. The places you frequent. Talk over any current struggles in this area.

9.  Discuss practical ways you can be more of a gentlemen and more pure in your relationships with women you encounter.

10. Have you shut down the demand in your life discussed on page 87? What do you have to do to shut down your demand? What steps can you take now?

Reading Psalm 51 on page 88 would be an awesome closing prayer.

## CHAPTER 8

# *LIVE PURE*
# STOP, DROP, & ROLL

*"Imaginary lovers, never turn you down.
When all the others turn you away, they're around."* [1]
—*Atlanta Rhythm Section*

While on a trip in Arizona, Matt George caught a rattlesnake. Holding the snake behind the head, he "kissed" it in front of all his friends. One of the guys said, "OK, man, you're being stupid. Put it down." George responded, "Oh, it's alright. I do this all the time." As he went to "kiss" the snake again, it pulled loose from his grip and bit him on the lip. He threw the snake down and one of his buddies killed it with his boot. As they waited for the ambulance, George's face started to swell and he began to cry out, "I'm going to die!"

Sheriff's Deputy Steven Johnson said he watched in the ambulance as George went limp and his eyes rolled back in his head. He was hospitalized in critical condition. [2] Do you think Matt George ever wanted to "kiss" another rattler?

There are people everywhere, including some of us, who have a different type of fang mark. There are so many of us that are poisoned in our hearts from the venom injected years ago by sexual liasons. There are people who are dead physically, emotionally, or sexually because of too many "snakebites," yet so many of us will just keep picking up snakes because we believe we are the exception to the rule and know what we're doing—like Matt George did. *"Oh, it's alright. I do this all the time."*

Many of us received our earliest impressions of sex from all the wrong sources and for all the wrong reasons. The first sexual discussions we heard were in locker rooms, school hallways, sleepovers, and hushed, giggling conversations between buddies. I can tell you personally that by the time I was sixteen, at least half of what I knew was just flat out bad info. My dad never had the "birds and bees" talk with me, so the real problem was that I didn't know what information I had that was right and what was wrong. It was a major mess for me. I would bet it was for a lot of you too. The enemy loves for our first impressions and mental imprints of sex to be wrong. It makes for a great start to living out our sex lives his way! Like the yard/weeds analogy helps us understand God's plan for ridding us of sin, maybe this analogy will help us understand God's plan for sex. … *"Robert, what's up with all the analogies?"* Well, we're guys. If we were women, we wouldn't need word pictures!

## SHE RAN CALLIN' WILDFIRE

It seems every year in the late spring and early summer, the news is filled with stories and aerial shots of California wildfires. These fires run … well, wild, burning quickly and destroying thousands of acres. They take lives, devastating families and homes. Inevitably, it seems that every year, we also hear that someone has intentionally set one of these wildfires. Some bonehead throws down a match into a pile of leaves or throws down his cigarette and destruction ensues. Sometimes it is intentional simply to watch the damage. (Those guys obviously don't have—or want—a garden hose handy like my dad did.)

Regardless of what we know about fire and it's potential for destruction, we still intentionally install a device in our homes that is made up of a metal box and a funnel of bricks. It may use logs or be fueled by gas, but it's called a fireplace. (Loosely translated, I believe the word means "place of fire." Don't you just love the English language?) The fireplace is a designated and contained space in our homes where we can build a fire for warmth and enjoyment.

Now, let's say I'm sitting at home one night and my wife says, "Honey, would you get a fire going?" I wouldn't grab a match and hold it to the rug and get a nice blaze going in the middle of the floor. That would be crazy. That would be wrong. That would confirm to my wife what I've given her plenty of reason to wonder about me anyway. That wouldn't be building a fire where fire was intended to be in my home. The right thing, but in the wrong place. Just like the wildfires in California. Isn't it interesting that a fire being set even just a few feet away from where it is supposed to be makes the difference in right and wrong, in delight and devastation? Fire is not bad. Fire in the wrong place is. It's all about location.

This is just like sex. God created sex, just like He created fire. He designed it for our enjoyment. He intended it to be an important part of our lives. BUT, He made a place for it. Just like the builder puts a place in our homes for a fire where it is contained and safe for our ultimate enjoyment, God made a place for sex where it is contained and safe for our ultimate enjoyment. Isn't it interesting how sex, even just a few miles away from where it is supposed to be, makes the difference in right and wrong, in delight and devastation? Sex is not bad. Sex in the wrong place is. It's all about location.

> SEX IS NOT BAD. SEX IN THE WRONG PLACE IS. IT'S ALL ABOUT LOCATION.

When a man, at any age, single or married, decides to take sex to the wrong location, he is in essence starting a wildfire that will burn up lives, and surely his own. Whether it's a high school senior who has just been told he has gotten his girlfriend pregnant, a college student who finds out he has genital herpes, or a man who watches his affair end his family, tell me that doesn't feel like a wildfire raging and devastating people's lives forever. People get burned. People feel burned. Men watch their lives and all they have worked for, go up in smoke just about as fast as the orgasm occurred. And all too often the innocent people burned are more likely to begin setting fires of their own, born from the pain created in them.

I referred earlier to John 10:10, but let's look at it now.

*"A thief comes to steal and kill and destroy, but I came to give life—life in all its fullness."* —*Jesus in John 10:10* NCV

I'm going to make a statement and it is going to sound crazy, (you're getting used to this, aren't you?) but hang with me. Ready? … Satan hates sex. … *"What? C'mon, Robert, our culture is rampant with sexual issues because he is using it everywhere!"* … Yeah, I know. But it is the misuse of God's gift that is rampant—not God's gift. God's gift of sex is still beautiful and holy for all those who use it in His way in the right location. Everywhere else, it is Satan using it to start wildfires. If he can use a precious gift, that God intended only for intimacy in marriage, to rob, kill, and destroy and have us throw God's gift back in His face, he loves that action—all day long!

I'm going to address yet another likely controversial topic here. I don't believe it is controversial regarding Scripture. I believe it lines up perfectly with Scripture and explains further why Satan hates sex. But it doesn't line up with our church culture. Here we go …

In the marriage bed, the intensity of feelings, love, and the pure, too-deep-for-words intimacy that happens between a husband and wife who are truly in love is an earthly reflection of the intensity and intimacy of what occurs between God's heart and our heart. When you are alone with God and He is so near to You and His presence is so strong, that level of relationship with Him is reflected in the sexual intimacy between a husband and wife. Sex—in its God-given location—is worship. … Now do you see why Satan hates it so much and wants to ruin it and destroy it for us all? If it is a picture of the depth of our relationship with God, if it has to do with the worship of a married couple toward their God, if it brings us life to the full, then no wonder the enemy makes it such a primary target for destruction?!

Once when I was teaching this concept to a men's group, there were also about five or six teenage boys, 16 and up, who were attending. When I made the statement that sex between a husband and wife can be an act of worship, one of the boy's mouths literally fell open. His eyes got big and I don't think he heard another word I said for about ten minutes. Now, that's funny to hear, but why did that young man react that way? Because so far in his young life, everything about sex was incredibly intriguing, but very dirty. The enemy's lies were his only imprint for sex. What would ever change that for him outside of proper Biblical teaching?

Now be honest. Even at your age, is your paradigm possibly close to the teenage boy's? As my wife and I have counseled couples for years, we've seen women time and time again who have grown up in Christian homes, and have been taught that sex—regardless of location—is nasty and immoral and can't see how marriage changes that. So guess what happens in the marriage? Single or married, I pray this book changes your paradigm of sex and God's intention for it.

If you're a dad, please talk to your son at the appropriate age about the Biblical view and purpose of sex. He needs the right info— from you. If you're a teenage son, cut your dad a little slack and let him talk to you.

## FROM PAGES TO PIXELS

If sex outside of marriage is an arsonist's wildfire, then pornography is the gasoline can in our culture. We have already covered this subject to some degree in the previous chapter through my two friends' testimonies and the plea to examine your own life in this area. But now we are going to delve more into where lust leads from a spiritual and emotional sense. And, it's not like this isn't really a hot button issue that doesn't warrant this much time and attention, right guys?

When I was a kid, the only way porn was potentially accessible was by finding a "men's magazine" that someone had thrown out or maybe some friend's dad or brother would have. When most of us got old enough to actually walk into a store and purchase a magazine, we might struggle with the humiliation and shame of asking for the title. And maybe we even actually cared what the anonymous store clerk might think of us. Bottom line is lots of obstacles, personally and culturally, used to be in place to keep many guys from porn. As you know, not so anymore.

It's really interesting today how most normal families would not even think of keeping a stack of pornography on the kitchen table, but they will put an unprotected computer in the family room. Internet access is not even something we pray about in this culture. It's considered a necessity. Food, water, shelter, Internet access. You know, the Big Four. I will admit that I finally, just last year, got Internet access in our home. (Yes, we have electricity and indoor bathrooms, in case you were wondering.) I worked with filters on my office computer until I was convinced one would work properly. But you should have seen the looks on people's faces up until last year when, with two teenage boys at home, people would find out we weren't "on-line." "What?!" they would say. "With two teenage boys, you don't have Internet access?!" To which I would respond, "That's exactly why we don't have Internet access!" We held out as long as we could, but Internet-based school homework was the final straw for me. We have filters on our computers and our phones as well. We also work hard to have open and honest dialogue on the tough topics, because a great "human filter" is a dad's strong, honest relationship with his child.

Over the years, I have talked with people who have been addicted to crack and meth. I have talked with people that have successfully beat these demons and restored their lives. I have also talked with guys that have been addicted to porn. There is no difference in the two, in regards to what it does to the person. It is an obsession and access becomes a necessity to survive. Time between needed fixes becomes shorter and shorter. Time away is often spent planning on the next fix. The hiding becomes more threatening and intense. The shame deepens as the addiction grows. Crack, meth, porn, all the same story. Porn is mental crack and emotional meth. Guys who would never consider doing drugs see porn differently, because it's socially acceptable to have a computer everywhere and to not have Internet access today is socially unacceptable. And, honestly, porn is becoming more accepted too. What was once considered "soft porn" is now known as the TV commercial.

If you could know now that your ten-year-old son would be addicted to porn by the time he was twenty, what steps would you take today to prevent that from happening? Maybe it's a good plan to go ahead and pretend he will be addicted and take the needed steps. And you guys with daughters? Your world is getting tougher too in this area. The stats are showing more and more girls are accessing and getting addicted to porn in two ways. First, they are reading pornographic stories, because that is more of what stimulates a female. (Who is the primary audience and draw for soap operas?) And two—they are looking at sites to find out what guys like, so they can recreate those acts to keep their boyfriends happy—the one male too many of them have come to believe they can't live without.[3]

Let's look at the typical cycle with pornography use. A guy feels alone, isolated, stressed, hurt, depressed, disappointed. He wants somewhere "safe" to go that will make him "feel better about himself." He turns to the females that will always take their clothes off, they never say no, they never have a headache, and they're always ready to go. They don't have to talk or require anything before sex. No commitment. No expectations. No matter what time of the day or night, they are there and ready. Surfing begins. Stimulation occurs. Relief through masturbation.

But what happens immediately afterwards, especially for the Christian man? Within seconds, guilt and condemnation flood in. The enemy begins the assault, "You call yourself a Christian? What

does your Jesus think about you now, huh? Big man of God, you are!"
Feelings of self-hate and sadness pervade the soul.

As this scenario continues and becomes more frequent, as we say
no to the Holy Spirit, the searing of our conscious begins. We become
calloused. We rationalize the behavior. We start to realize it is controlling us, rather than us controlling it. That is known as addiction.

I believe Satan gets two great thrills out of a Christian man engag-
ing in this sin. First, the sin itself. Then second, the opportunity to
hurl accusations and condemnation at him. Even if it is days or weeks
before another sexual sin occurs, he loves to whisper in your ear. "Hey,
remember when you did that? That was horrible. You should be so
ashamed. That's really who you are, you know. You're not the great
Christian at all." The accusations can be fun for the enemy for a very
long time. Then when he gets bored with this part, he goes right back
around to the temptation again. Definite cycle. I believe one of his favorite pastimes is messing with Christian men. What else does he have
to look forward to with us? His fate is sealed and he's read the Book.
What better for him to do than to cripple the very guys who will obey
and serve the King of Kings? But instead of watching him pick off our
brothers one at a time, why don't we circle up, get a game plan, put on
the armor, and fight back?

## THE "M" WORD

Okay, I skirted around this earlier, but now we're going to deal
with it. ... Masturbation—one of the many topics that churches,
pastors, Christian publishers, authors, speakers, and ministries won't
address for fear of offending Christians. And God forbid we ever get
controversial following Jesus! For some reason, the church just hasn't
wanted to address sexual issues in a forthright manner. There are just
some topics that we have decided shouldn't be discussed. We're just
too darn spiritual for that! The church has this big "rug" and we just

love to sweep all those things under it. Meanwhile, the issues we won't address are destroying our brothers and sisters left and right in their own private Hells. We won't talk about it, so they don't feel

GOD IS NEVER GLORIFIED IN THE CHURCH'S SILENCE.

they can get help, so guess who wins there? Our enemy. God is never glorified in the church's silence. So, here we go … again …

First, let's define masturbation. … *"Uh, are you kidding, Robert? I think we know what it means."* … Yeah, I know you do, but here's why we have to define it. Because people put masturbation in the category of "Things the Bible Doesn't Speak To, Therefore We Obviously Are Able To Do Without Consequence." Look up masturbation in your Bible's concordance and you will find nada. Zero. That is true with a lot of issues. So, we have to take all Scripture on the area of sex and apply them to this topic.

Let's go with the definition of masturbation as "sex with yourself." If the physical act of sex is genital arousal for the goal of climax, then I believe masturbation qualifies as sex. The social connotation of the word is that you do it alone. Alone would qualify as "outside of marriage" or outside of the sanctity of "the marriage bed," so let's apply that definition to this passage.

*There's more to sex than mere skin on skin. Sex is as much spiritual mystery as physical fact. As written in Scripture, "The two become one." Since we want to become spiritually one with the Master, we must not pursue the kind of sex that avoids commitment and intimacy, leaving us more lonely than ever—the kind of sex that can never "become one." There is a sense in which sexual sins are different from all others. In sexual sin we violate the sacredness of our own bodies, these bodies that were made for God-given and God-modeled love, for "becoming one" with another.*
—*1 Corinthians 6:16–18* MSG

Here's some questions as we work through and apply this passage:

1. Do you agree that masturbation is simply "mere skin on skin"?
2. When you make love to your wife (or if you're single, as you look forward to that day), do you sense (or anticipate) the "spiritual mystery" in those moments? Conversely, do you sense any "spiritual mystery" in masturbation or is it more just "physical fact"?
3. Does masturbation "avoid commitment"?
4. Does masturbation "avoid intimacy"?
5. When masturbation is completed, does it leave you "more lonely than ever"?
6. Is masturbation the kind of sex that can "become one" or "never become one?"
7. If God created your sexual being solely to enjoy and be enjoyed by a spouse, is masturbation "a violation of the sacredness of your own body?"
8. Do you think masturbation is an example of "God-given and God-modeled love?"

Here's another major spiritual issue with masturbation. This goes back to our discussion of Jesus' definition of lust and purity. Likely 99.99 percent of the time masturbation involves the imagining of a sex act with someone. If you're single, that is sex outside of marriage. If you're married, that is adultery. Every scenario applied to the mental aspect of masturbation causes this to violate Jesus' adultery Scriptures.

I have heard men confess that when their wives put them off for too long that they will masturbate, but imagine sex with their wife. Most of the time that confession comes in the form of a question intended to ask: "So, that's okay, right?" Well, go back to the above passage and eight questions for that answer.

There was a time in our culture when masturbation was a taboo topic. Not so anymore. The culture has made it a commonality and, honestly, made it the equivalent of a "harmless joke." It is no longer considered a temptation, but an assumption.

If you are a dad with a son, you have got to discuss this issue with him. Yeah, it is veeerrrrry awkward to bring up for the first time. Believe me, I know. But, over time, that level of open and honest communication can make your boys into godly men, who can understand that no subject is unapproachable with you and nothing is impossible for God. One of my hopes with this book is that men might go through it with their sons and all the "hot button topics" can be brought up and discussed as a natural progression of moving through the book.

## INPUT & INTAKE

Let's go back to our past discussion regarding the mind and repeat a very basic, simple principle. What we put into our minds is what will come out of our thoughts, and eventually our actions. As simple as it is, as guys we forget that truth all too often. I know I do. We think we can avoid Scripture, take in whatever we want, but then get frustrated with ourselves for not becoming godlier. This is a very vicious cycle for far too many of us.

To be clear, what would happen if you have been on a steady diet of lust and porn, then stopped and began to spend that same amount of time in God's Word? Do you think that would change anything? Would thoughts become different? Would actions be different?

We can't constantly fill our minds with everything but God, and then expect to be godly men. Please prayerfully and carefully read these passages below in light of all we have discussed.

*"Don't allow love to turn into lust, setting off a downhill slide into sexual promiscuity, filthy practices, or bullying greed. Though some tongues just love the taste of gossip, those who follow Jesus have better uses for language than that. Don't talk dirty or silly. That kind of talk doesn't fit our style. Thanksgiving is our dialect." —Ephesians 5:3–4* MSG

*"Your old life is dead. Your new life, which is your real life—even though invisible to spectators—is with Christ in God. He is your life. When Christ (your real life, remember) shows up again on this earth, you'll show up, too—the real you, the glorious you. Meanwhile, be content with obscurity, like Christ.*

*And that means killing off everything connected with that way of death: sexual promiscuity, impurity, lust, doing whatever you feel like whenever you feel like it, and grabbing whatever attracts your fancy. That's a life shaped by things and feelings instead of by God. It's because of this kind of thing that God is about to explode in anger. It wasn't long ago that you were doing all that stuff and not knowing any better. But you know better now, so make sure it's all gone for good." —Colossians 3:3–8a* MSG

In closing—and to apply another sports metaphor—you know a team can't win a game if the defense is always on the field. Through the power of Christ in this area of purity, it is entirely possible to finally get the defense off the field for a while and let the offense take over and put some points on the board for the Kingdom. You can win this game! Maybe you have told yourself you can't. Maybe the enemy keeps telling you that you can't. But you can address your hurts and needs, face your motives, take your thoughts captive, and end the actions that are hurting your soul, while taking up actions that glorify God and satisfy your spirit!

That is exactly what the last chapter in this *Live Pure* section of *The Knight's Code* deals with—taking action steps to move forward in Christ.

## DISCUSSION QUESTIONS

1.  Why do we as guys so often think we are going to be the exception to the rule?

2.  Discuss how you developed your sexual paradigm. Where did you learn "the facts of life?" Was it right or wrong?

3.  Discuss the sex/fire analogy. Have you ever been burned in a wildfire?

4.  Talk about the "Satan hates sex" concept. Discuss how he would hate and want to destroy what God created for our good and enjoyment.

5.  Discuss the concept on Page 93 of sex in the marriage bed being an act of worship. Why is that idea often controversial in our church circles?

6.  Why do you think the enemy seems to have such a stronghold and plan of attack in our sexual lives?

7.  Why do you think masturbation is such a taboo topic inside church circles?

8.  Discuss the 1 Corinthians 6:16–18 passage on Page 98 and the eight questions that follow.

9.  Read Colossians 3:3–8a on Page 101 and discuss the things that Paul tells us to "kill off."

10. Discuss the closing paragraph and the offense/defense metaphor on Page 101. Why do so many of us guys have the defense on the field most of the time? What do you need to do to put your offense to work for Christ?

    Close in prayer.

CHAPTER 9

# *LIVE PURE*
## SEVEN STEPS TO PURITY

*"My mind is dull and faded from these years of buy and sell.*
*My eyes have seen the glory of this hollow modern shell."*
*And sex is a grand production, but I'm bored with that as well."*
*Lord, save me from myself."* [1]
*—Jon Foreman*

We're going to jump straight into the practical points of this chapter. Here are seven steps to purity in your life.

**1.  First, You Must Deal With the Sin.**

In AA (Alcoholics Anonymous), members are told that first they must acknowledge they have a problem. Specifically, Step One states, "We admitted we were powerless over alcohol—that our lives had become unmanageable." Interestingly, Step Two and Three have to do with turning life and will over to God to be restored.[2] That is true for us all. We must recognize sin exists and want to change the behavior. We must agree with God that we have wronged Him. We must agree with Him that it is bad for us. That sense of conviction should drive us back to God, not away from Him.

*Godly sorrow brings repentance that leads to salvation and leaves no regret, but worldly sorrow brings death. —2 Corinthians 7:10 NIV*

*The Lord is not slow in keeping his promise, as some understand slowness. He is patient with you, not wanting anyone to perish, but everyone to come to repentance.* — *2 Peter 3:9* NIV

### 2.   Confess Your Sin/Disobedience

*If we confess our sins, he is faithful and just and will forgive our sins and purify us from all unrighteousness.* —*1 John 1:9* NIV

Look at what we must do in this agreement: Confess to Christ. Then look at what Christ will do: Be faithful. Be just. Forgive us. Purify us. From how much unrighteousness? All of it. His answer is "yes," we just have to ask the question.

### 3.   Un-isolate Yourself

Our culture encourages isolation in general, but particularly among men. There are a lot of men today that are not strongly connected to anyone. If they got into trouble at 3 p.m. or 3 a.m., they would have difficulty figuring out who to call for help. Often men are even isolated inside their own families, living in the same house, but not emotionally engaged on any level.

*There was a man all alone; he had neither son nor brother. There was no end to his toil, yet his eyes were not content with his wealth. "For whom am I toiling," he asked, "and why am I depriving myself of enjoyment?" This too is meaningless—a miserable business!* —*Ecclesiastes 4:8* NIV

Un-isolation begins by reaching out to your family first, and then to Christian brothers. An isolated man is a prideful man. You will have to willfully drop your pride and ego. Let your guard down. You will have to make an effort to connect. To have friends, you must, first, be one. Become the man that you would want as a friend. Yes, it will be hard to be vulnerable, but it is necessary for change to come. You have to open your heart.

> YES, IT WILL BE HARD TO BE VULNERABLE, BUT IT IS NECESSARY FOR CHANGE TO COME. YOU HAVE TO OPEN YOUR HEART.

Every man that I have helped come out of deep issues or addiction was isolated. The healthier he got, the more he opened up to God and others, and the more un-isolated he became. Once you begin to un-isolate, then you need …

### 4. Accountability

In order to stop drinking, why do AA members have to commit to come regularly to the meetings? Because the meetings create accountability.[3] The meetings are the catalyst for change and victory. "If I drink during the week, I *have* to tell the group. If I don't drink during the week, I *get* to tell the group."

Continuing on in Ecclesiastes 4 …

*Two are better than one, because they have a good return for their work: If one falls down, his friend can help him up. But pity the man who falls and has no one to help him up! Also, if two lie down together, they will keep warm. But how can one keep warm alone? Though one may be overpowered, two can defend themselves. A cord of three strands is not quickly broken. —Ecclesiastes 4:9–12 NIV*

Accountability is simply helping each other stand strong, defeat sin, and live for Christ. If you have (1) admitted a problem, (2) confessed to God, then go to a Christian brother—or two—and ask for help and prayer. When you're tempted, you need someone to talk it through with. Sometimes just calling the person will stop the temptation. Or text or e-mail, or whatever you have to do, whatever method is available to you. But sometimes, you have to ask for help to not go through with it. I call it "talking you down out of the tree." Then when you do sin, it can stop the condemnation attack if you go ahead and tell your friend and confess. Regardless, this is the key to lasting success over sin.

I have a young friend who is a Christian in a mainstream rock band. They have a record deal and travel all over the world. He can end up in some interesting situations. He can end up in some compromising positions. Almost every night on the road brings that scenario. We have spent hours on the phone doing exactly what I am talking about here. His flesh has the opportunity, but his spirit doesn't want to go there. At times, you can hear the battle raging in his words. Being honest, we have won some and lost some, but overall, he has been able to make it through fairly unscathed in a crazy world only because of accountability.

Remember the story of the couple in Chapter 3? When my friend's affair and porn addiction came out, he handed over his computer. He was self-employed and didn't require it a lot to accomplish his job, so he used his parent's during that season only when they were present. It was many months before he had access to his own computer again. Accountability on this level is a major reason that he was restored and is now living in a successful marriage. I have received a lot of personal criticism in the past for stressing the importance of accountability among believers, but the typical, "Hey buddy, how's it going? I'll pray for you" would not have cut it for my friend to stop and restore. And he now helps other guys be accountable that have and are struggling. Why? Because he knows what they do—and don't—need.

Gordon McDonald was a popular author, pastor, speaker, and Christian leader throughout the 1980s. He publicly admitted to an affair that had lasted for years. When asked what led him to that point, he answered, "I was desperately weary in spirit and body. I was working harder and enjoying it less. I now realize I was lacking accountability through personal relationships. We have to have friendships where one man regularly looks another man in the eye and asks hard questions about our moral life, lust, ambitions, and ego."[4]

John Bisagno has been one of the most successful pastors in Southern Baptist history. He tells the story of when he was about to finish college and was having dinner at his fiancée's house one night. After supper, he was talking out on the porch with his future father-in-law who had been in ministry for years.

"John, as you get ready to enter the ministry, I want to give you some advice," the minister told the younger man. "Make sure that you keep your heart close to Jesus every day. It's a long way from here to where you are going to go, and Satan's in no hurry to get you. It has been my observation that just one out of ten who start out in full time service for the Lord at 21 are still on track by the age of 65. They get shot down morally, with discouragement, liberal theology, with making money, but for one reason or another nine out of ten fall out." Bisagno was shocked. "I just can't believe that!" he said. "That's impossible. That just can't be true."

Bisagno told how he went home, how he took one of those blank pages in the back of his Scofield Reference Bible and wrote down the names of 24 young men who were his peers. These were young men that were also sold out for Jesus Christ. These were the committed young preachers who would make an impact for the Lord in their generation. Bisagno then related the following with a sigh, "From time to time as the years have gone by, I've had to turn back to that page in my Bible and cross out a name. I wrote down those 24 names when I was just 20 years of age. Thirty-three years later, there are only three names remaining of the original 24." One of the three was Bisagno himself.[5]

I heard a man give his testimony at a church where he explained the way his wife figured out he was having an affair was by looking at his calendar. She asked him to explain where he was at certain times while away from the house and on certain trips. Bottom line is there was too much time away from home and too much unaccounted time.

Think about it. Where would any of our Armed Forces be without accountability? Doctors? Lawyers? Our judicial system? What keeps everyone from driving 100 miles per hour on the highway or taking whatever they want, from whomever they want, whenever they want? Accountability. It is built into our lives all around us, so it makes sense to build it in intentionally on a spiritual level for the sake of survival over the long run.

### 5.  Develop Principles for Offense and Defense

B*ut principled people hold tight, keep a firm grip on life, sure that their clean, pure hands will get stronger and stronger!* —*Job 17:9* MSG

*A thick bankroll is no help when life falls apart, but a principled life can stand up to the worst.* —*Proverbs 11:4* MSG

*The thinking of principled people makes for justice; the plots of degenerates corrupt.* —*Proverbs 12:5* MSG

*Listen carefully to my wisdom; take to heart what I can teach you. You'll treasure its sweetness deep within; you'll give it bold expression in your speech. To make sure your foundation is trust in God, I'm laying it all out right now just for you. I'm giving you thirty sterling principles—tested guidelines to live by. Believe me—these are truths that work, and will keep you accountable to those who sent you.* —*Proverbs 22:17* MSG

A principle is a simple boundary you set for yourself for the purpose of protection (defense) or growth (offense). Some principles are just for a season, while some are for a lifetime. Now that you have confessed your sin and see your areas of shortcoming, look at any situation or place or person that causes you to be tempted. Put principles in place to protect you from that circumstance. Then give your principles to your accountability partners. You should also give a list of your principles to your wife. If you have an older son, it would be cool to share appropriate ones with him too.

Some examples:

**Problem:** When that certain client comes into town, he always wants to frequent a certain place after work that you know you don't need to go to, but you feel obligated to take him. If you are honest, you look forward to him coming, because it gives you an excuse to go.

**Principle:** Don't go to any place where temptation is a given.

**Position:** Just be up-front and tell him you have made a spiritual commitment and you can't do that anymore. Tell him you'll be great to go to dinner, but nothing else. Tell him if he wants to go on without you, you don't judge him. And who knows? Maybe he wouldn't go if you didn't?

If you are still tempted, maybe you need to ask your boss to re-assign that client to someone else. Remember Jesus' words—if your right eye causes you to sin, cut it out. It would cost you to lose an eye. Taking action will likely always cost you something. If it came down to losing that client or your family, which would you choose? Based on your answer, do what you need to do.

<u>Plan:</u> Tell your Christian buddies about this situation and what your position is. Then allow them to ask you about it and hold you to your own word.

Here's another scenario:

<u>Problem:</u> There is a female at your work that gets flirty with you and you find yourself getting flirty back all too often. In fact, you go back and forth between scared and excited of where this could go.

<u>Principle:</u> No flirting with anyone but your wife.

<u>Position:</u> If it is possible to end all communication with her, that would be best. If you have to communicate for the business, then only talk with this woman in a group of people. If you have to talk with her, take a buddy with you. If everyone walks off or she is alone, you just keep moving. Don't look, don't talk, just keep on walking. You don't have to be rude, but you do have to change the behavior. Bottom line is you're not playing the game anymore.

<u>Plan:</u> Tell your buddies about this woman and have them ask you periodically if you are staying clear of her and dealing with her only in a professional and Christian manner.

Let's give a positive example (offense) where you want to grow.

<u>Problem:</u> You've never felt comfortable leading your family in a devotional or prayer time, but you want to start. You're concerned that your wife will think this is too little, too late and you wonder if your kids will listen to you and cut you some slack.

**Principle:** Lead my family in a weekly devotional and prayer time.

**Position:** Talk the conviction over with your wife. Tell her your motive and goal, along with your fears. Share your heart. Agree on a night and time and tell the kids. Then make sure you follow through and you're prepared. Keep it simple and short at first. Know that the enemy is going to try and make you feel inept and stupid, but that's not true and you have to keep trying. For some reason, that is usually what he does when men first try this with their families. If you get serious about leading your family spiritually, you will get the enemy's attention.

**Plan:** Tell your buddies your plan. Have them pray for you at the time you will be with your family. Give them a report on how it went, what you did well, and what you want to improve on. Have them hold you accountable to the schedule you set and if you miss a time, you will get right back to it the next time.

Now that I have given you some examples, hopefully you get the idea. Take some time to write out any problem areas you have now and then write out some principles, positions and plans. Getting a positive plan of attack will bring you closer than ever to victory and that is going to feel really good!

### 6. Detox Your Mind

If you do a detox or detoxification diet, you stop eating all the bad stuff and you only eat small portions of good stuff. A typical detox diet involves only drinking water and fruit juice, while eating vegetables and nuts for a designated time, usually under the supervision of a doctor or nutritionist. The bottom line is you radically change what you put into your body in order to cleanse your system.

A mental and spiritual detox involves radically changing what you put into your mind and heart. Write down anything that is placing negative, tempting, or anti-Christian images in front of you. Computer, phone, TV, movies, magazines, books, certain people, and certain situations. Set a specific span of time for you to stop or seriously limit your time with these elements. For example, between work and outside of work, you figure you waste a couple of hours a day on the computer. Cut out all that use for a while. Do you tend to watch TV shows that create temptation? Stop them for a time. You and your wife, or maybe a buddy, aren't very discriminating on the movies you go see? Stop that for a season.

The goal here is to disrupt your normal patterns, so you can give your mind and soul a break from your usual diet of input. Replace as much of this time as possible with time in God's Word and in prayer. You may find within a week to two weeks, you have started some new, healthier habits. You may find that there are some things you can easily live without and improve your quality of life.

*For we are the temple of the living God. As God has said: "I will live with them and walk among them, and I will be their God, and they will be my people." "Therefore come out from them and be separate, says the Lord. Touch no unclean thing, and I will receive you." "I will be a Father to you, and you will be my sons and daughters, says the Lord Almighty." Since we have these promises, dear friends, let us purify ourselves from everything that contaminates body and spirit, perfecting holiness out of reverence for God. —2 Corinthians 6:16b–7:1 NIV*

The spirit of this passage from Paul is obedience and action for the sake of holiness. That is what this detox concept is all about.

Here's an example of a detox decision that developed into a principle for me: For years, I always got a Sunday paper and would read through most sections. It usually took about two hours on Sunday afternoon or evening. I started noticing that when I had finished reading, my spirit was troubled for a while. Sometimes I even felt stressed out. I realized reading the paper with all the negative news and sensationalized stories were not a good thing for me. I decided to stop getting the Sunday paper. I also ended up buying less stuff by not looking at the store flyers. And it's not like I don't get news from other sources throughout the week. I have found much better things to do with that two hours on Sunday.

### 7. The Promise of Replacement

Regardless of how godly we become here, we also remain human. If we begin to look at our lives through the filter of all these things we must stop or no longer do, we will eventually either exasperate ourselves or become legalistic or both. I believe that for everything God asks us to give up for Him, He will replace it with something so much better. That is a clear pattern of Scripture. That said, we must be proactive to cooperate with Him. Here's an example.

If a drinker comes to Christ and decides he must now quit drinking, if he has been spending two hours every night at a bar, he better figure out what he's going to do with his new-found two hours or he'll just end up back at the bar again! We must pray and ask God to help us replace the things we give up with good things from Him. He will help us replace our stuff with His stuff, but we have to ask Him, listen, and look for His answers. Allow the Lord to put what He wants in place of whatever we're giving up. (Remember—pulling weeds leaves a hole.) Here's another example for the single guys.

The girl you have been dating is not helping you live pure. You have talked to her about your sexual convictions, but that seems to just fuel the fire. You know you have to break up with her. You get accountability to break up, stay away, and stop communication. You hung out with her a minimum of 15 hours a week. Decide immediately what you will fill that time with. Is there a hobby or sport you have wanted to learn? A buddy or two you have been neglecting because of her? Is there a volunteering opportunity you've always said you would like to help with? Bottom line is if you find yourself sitting alone with an extra 15 hours on your hands, there is a strong likelihood you will phone her up or get into trouble of some other kind. So you must plan on doing good. Pray and ask the Lord for guidance on what to do.

Married guys, you can apply this same concept to anything you give up. We may have less time to get in trouble, but we've proven over and over again that it won't always stop us.

This concept that God not only will, but wants to, give us new things from Him is seen throughout Scripture. Here is a beautiful statement of love and promise that God made to Israel and makes available to you and I today. Look at the number of offers made to us just in three simple verses.

*I will sprinkle clean water on you, and you will be clean; I will cleanse you from all your impurities and from all your idols. I will give you a new heart and put a new spirit in you; I will remove from you your heart of stone and give you a heart of flesh. And I will put my Spirit in you and move you to follow my decrees and be careful to keep my laws.*
—*Ezekiel 36:25–27 NIV*

## ATTITUDE REFLECT LEADERSHIP, CAP'N

As we get serious about changing our actions, this will, by default cause us to work on our attitudes. We have all seen how when we are unhappy with our lives and conviction is constantly hammering us, then we usually have really crappy attitudes too. Our attitudes and our actions are tied together in our souls. One affects the other. One creates the other.

There is a place in us where our flesh is constantly at work, yet simultaneously the Lord is constantly at work too. In our motives. This is the classic scene where the angel is on one shoulder and a devil on the other and both are whispering in our ears.

We talked before about how all our decisions are born in our souls, but the embryo from which all decisions grow is called a motive.

Think about a murder scene. The police stake off the area. Make the chalk lines around the body. Begin to scour the scene for clues and evidence. But quickly, the | THE EMBRYO FROM WHICH ALL DECISIONS GROW IS CALLED A MOTIVE.

lead detective will begin to look for who had the strongest motive for this person to be dead. We hear it all the time. Someone is dead, but the motive was money. Someone is dead, but the motive was jealousy. Someone is dead, but the motive was concealing identity. The end result is the same, but the driving force behind the action is vastly different. Motive.

Then here is where it can get really complicated. We can do something that looks very nice, very good, and harmless, but we do it with completely the wrong motive. We give someone a high compliment, but the motive is to manipulate that person. Why? To get them to do what we want. We buy someone something they really want and it makes them very happy, but the motive is to get them to give us something that is far more valuable to us than the money we spent.

There are men that, rather than just be up-front and honest about what they need to be done or want, will manipulate people through their words. So they operate in what appears to be a very honest manner through very dishonest motives. They get things done by moving, shaking, and maneuvering, while at the same time avoiding honest communication.

Gentlemen—real and godly purity is driven by motives. What is it that drove Christ in the Garden, throughout the trials, the beatings, the whipping with the cat-of-nine-tails, the walk up to Golgotha with the cross, the nails through the wrists, the nails through the feet, and the hours in agony trying not to suffocate hanging on the cross? What drove Him to give up His life to the Father as a final sacrifice for all sin? ... The answer: His motive of love for you and I!

All we can be capable of in our sin, death, and flesh is more sin, death, and flesh. We are not able to produce life, love, joy, peace, patience, kindness, goodness, gentleness, or self-control. We cannot have pure motives, attitudes, or actions in our own power and strength. Christ offers the opportunity to change all that.

Gentlemen, God knows the root of our actions are our motives. So He is after our motives. To make them His. To make them pure. To radically change us from the inside out. To make all things new.

We have spent four chapters looking in deep detail about this issue of purity. It is vitally important that you grasp that a pure life is possible in Christ and only in Christ. There is no point in challenging you to speak truth, right wrongs, and truly follow Christ the King in freedom, if you cannot first strive to live in purity. And again, let me be clear that I am not speaking of perfection, only of surrender and obedience.

When we are impure—and we will be—we simply confess to Him, He cleans us up, and we get right back to a life of following Him with the passion to be pure. To *"be holy as he is holy."*

Pray with me: *Merciful and gracious God, we thank You that You have provided a path to purity, in our actions, attitudes, and even our motives. Give us the sense to surrender when we are defeated, the wisdom to turn to You and obey, the grace to forgive ourselves as you forgive us, and the boldness to move forward in Your freedom. May each day bring greater victory over the places in us where we have allowed the enemy to set up camp. May we defeat and remove him from our lives. Then please take possession of every part of our hearts, so we can know You in the fullness and intimacy that You dreamed of when You hung on the cross and redeemed our sin. Give us the daily desire to seek Your purity in our lives. Now, as we move forward into pursuing truth in our souls, help us to understand and discern what Your Word call us to. In the Name of Christ, the King. Amen.*

## DISCUSSION QUESTIONS

1.  Do you know anyone who is an AA success story? Share.

2.  Step One (p. 103): Why are conviction and confession often so hard for us to deal with? Why do we often deny we have issues?

3.  Step Two (p. 104): Why do you think God would ask us to simply confess, while He agrees to do so much for us?

4.  Step Three (p. 104): Rate your level of isolation with "1 being rarely alone and life is an open book" to "10 being totally alone and closed up." Explain your answer.

5.  Step Four (p. 105): Do you think of accountability as a positive or negative term? Why? How can we create more protection for each other?

6.  Step Five (p. 108): Discuss the Principle examples given in this section. Discuss some of your own temptations and potential solutions.

7.  Step Six (pp. 110–111): Discuss the mental/spiritual detox concept. What should you consider giving up for a time?

8.  Step Seven (p. 112): Give an example of something God has asked you to give up, but has replaced it with something of Him that is much better.

9.  How do you think God can get to the core of our decisions—our motives? How can He change us that deeply? Has He ever changed one of your motives?

10. Why do you think our level of purity is the doorway to speaking truth and righting wrongs?

    Close in prayer.

CHAPTER 10

# *SPEAK TRUE*
# MY STUPID MOUTH

*"My stupid mouth has got me in trouble
I said too much again …
How could I forget, Mama said 'think before speaking'
No filter in my head, what's a boy to do?
Guess I better find one soon"* [1]
—John Mayer

I must echo John Mayer's confession in his song. I, too, have a stupid mouth. And all the guys I know, well … they all have stupid mouths too. In fact, I don't know a single guy who doesn't have a decent size list of stupid mouth stories. How many times have you been telling stories with some buddies and one of you says while laughing or in shock, "Man, I cannot believe you said that! What were you thinking?!" I'm going to go out on a limb here and bet that you have a stupid mouth like me. … Oh, was that offensive? … I'm sorry. … See how quickly it can happen when you suffer from this?

As guys, we can get in trouble often with what we say … and even with what we *don't* say. I opened the first chapter of the book with a passage from Romans 7. If we apply Paul's concept of behavioral paradox to speech, he might say: "The very thing I shouldn't say, I say, and the very thing I should say, I don't say."

What we must quickly realize is that, as men, our mouths need help. Our mouths desperately need balance. Again, and I understand

I am being repetitious throughout these chapters, but this is exactly why we need a Savior and a Lord. One of the major parts of us that needs to be redeemed *daily* is our mouth!

The first time I heard the lyrics from John Mayer's song, I thought to myself, "Man, what guts this guy has to be so straight up about the problem with our tongues, and he even directed it at himself. Good for him!" Now that Mr. Mayer has been around for a few years, everyone knows he is an eccentric genius and a brilliant musician, but we have also seen why he warned us about his speech. But every time I listen to "Stupid Mouth," I don't think about him, I think about my own issue with my own tongue!

How many times have you wished you had a filter that would stop thoughts between your brain and your tongue and subject them to some sort of censoring to deem whether they are fit to proceed out of your mouth? For me, it is multiple times a day. See, I don't just have trouble with *what* I say, but *how* I say it. This whole speech thing gets really tricky, doesn't it? That's exactly why after we begin our journey toward purity, the next thing to battle is our tongue.

*The tongue also is a fire, a world of evil among the parts of the body. It corrupts the whole person, sets the whole course of his life on fire, and is itself set on fire by hell. All kinds of animals, birds, reptiles and creatures of the sea are being tamed and have been tamed by man, but no man can tame the tongue. It is a restless evil, full of deadly poison. With the tongue we praise our Lord and Father, and with it we curse men, who have been made in God's likeness. Out of the same mouth come praise and cursing. My brothers, this should not be. Can both fresh water and salt water flow from the same spring? My brothers, can a fig tree bear olives, or a grapevine bear figs? Neither can a salt spring produce fresh water.* —James 3:6–12 NIV*

*"I will watch my ways [purity] and keep my tongue [speech] from sin; I will put a muzzle on my mouth ... "* —David in Psalm 39:1 NIV*

Hit your thumb with a hammer lately? Gotten cut off in traffic? Had a co-worker get in your face? Someone in your family tick you off? The mouth is an amazing gauge of our purity at any given moment, is it not?

## Overflow

Let's roll into *Speak True* with a knight's tale:

King Philip II of France was holding court in Gatinais when the news reached him of the death of William Marshall. The king took care to wait until all had finished eating, then before the watchful asembly, he said, "Have you heard what this messenger has told me? He has come to tell me that the Earl of Pembroke, William, that loyal man, who was valiant and wise, is dead and buried. In our time, there was no better knight anywhere, and none who was more diligent in arms. William Marshall was, in my judgment, the most loyal man and true that I have ever known, in any country where I have been."[2]

William Marshall died in May of 1219 at 73 years old. In May of 1217, he led the attack for England at Lincoln Castle, and in September of that same year, negotiated the Treaty of Lambeth. The defeated king in the war? King Philip II of France.[3]

Oh, for us all to live a life so full of honor and integrity that when we die, even our enemies have nothing but good to say! You can't gain a reputation like this without also being known for speaking the truth.

Recently, my family was driving up Monteagle Mountain in Tennessee and in numerous places along the way, there were huge, flowing waterfalls coming straight out of the rocks right beside the road. The water was gushing from the rocks, crashing down the cliff, pouring into a huge culvert, and flowing down the mountain. It was powerful. It was beautiful. You could not see the source, but you could see what was flowing from the source.

*The good man brings good things out of the good stored up in his heart, and the evil man brings evil things out of the evil stored up in his heart. For out of the overflow of his heart his mouth speaks. —Jesus in Luke 6:45 NIV*

So, we are like those rocks. Jesus says that our mouths speak what overflows from our hearts. Isn't it interesting how good that overflow can be at times? How it can bless those who hear it. How it can bless us for speaking it. The good stored up in our heart.

Then isn't it strange how moments later we can curse someone and kill with our words? The evil stored up in our heart.

The bottom line is we are going to "gush" something. The question is the source from which it flows. King Philip couldn't help but respect William Marshall for what flowed from his life.

As I apply Luke 6:45 to my own mouth, I am good one minute and evil the next. The goal and hope, however, is that the good is slowly prevailing over the evil day by day, as my heart, and then my mouth, come under the submission of Christ. And this is an ongoing, life-long process, not an event.

Gentlemen, I want you to look at your own mouth—words, tones, and intentions—as an overflow from your heart. That is exactly what Jesus said to do.

So with that understood, what is regularly overflowing from your heart? I'm not talking about how you *think* you are communicating. Or how you assume you are sounding to people. What vibe do you regularly give off in your communication? What is your source? I'm talking about day in and day out, what tends to overflow from you? How would your wife answer that? Your kids? Friends? Parents? Co-workers? Boss? Employees? Clients? Pastor?

Now, as I have stated repeatedly in past chapters, questions and challenges like this are not intended to create guilt or condemnation, but simply for you to make a personal, honest evaluation of where you are with your speech. In this book, we are taking life apart one major segment at a time. We can't address our issues in any of these areas until we understand and admit what is wrong and what we must improve on. This is exactly why the average guy fights going to counseling. This stuff is hard to do and difficult to face.

*The mouth of the righteous man utters wisdom, and his tongue speaks what is just. —Psalm 37:30 NIV*

Learning the balance of speech—when to use it and when not to use it—is the gaining of wisdom. That balance is available through Christ.

## INTROS & EXTROS

One of the biggest defenses I hear from guys when speech becomes the topic is this: "Well, but my personality is … "

I didn't fill in the blank because it doesn't matter if you say you're an extrovert or an introvert or how much of one you are. This cannot be used as an excuse to not allow Christ to become the Lord of your mouth! The Lord of the overflow from your heart! But lots of guys do just that. They try and excuse a stupid mouth with personality type. They hide under the guise of "well, that's just how I am."

Yes, Christ gave each of us a very distinct and unique personality and He wants us to be who He has made us to be. However, as disciples of Jesus, He should overtake our personality—whether extroverted or introverted—and be the driving force behind our life and speech. You see it? Our personality should not be the gatekeeper of our mouth, but Christ. Extroverts can learn when to shut up and listen. Introverts can learn when to speak up and say what's on their minds. He becomes the Source of the overflow, not our flesh. Our personality becomes the unique way that we look while being Jesus, when our mouth is under His submission. That puts a whole different spin and responsibility on us. So "Dude, I can't help it. It's just the way I am,"

> OUR PERSONALITY SHOULD NOT BE THE GATEKEEPER OF OUR MOUTH, BUT CHRIST.

doesn't cut it anymore. And you already know that, "But honey, I can't help it. It's just the way I am," doesn't work at home, does it?

I am classified by every personality test as an introvert. If my wife and I go to a social gathering where there are a number of people that I don't know, I will stay back and size up the room before I engage anyone. I am much more likely to wait for someone to come to me. It takes me a while to get comfortable and talk freely. I will be polite. I will be nice. But I stay back.

However, those who know me well, or would watch me teach or lead worship, would never think of me as an introvert. Why? In order to be an effective minister of the Gospel, I have had to learn to place my personality under the Lordship of Christ and allow Him to empower me to do His will and work—in His way, not mine. As an introvert, that is uncomfortable—a lot—but it is not about me any longer. When God invited me to minister, I don't recall Him giving me a personality test to be certain I could handle the job. Or passing me up because I didn't have the right temperament for the assignment. He wants to continually use me and stretch me in who I am. That just requires me being available, not so much being able. Same goes for you. And our level of obedience at any given moment dictates our success.

A counselor friend of mine, with a very similar personality as me, calls our experience, "Becoming extroverted for the sake of the Kingdom." See, I have to work to allow extroverted behavior to accomplish what God needs me to do. That causes me to have to rely heavily upon Him, because it is not at all natural. For it to be supernatural, He has to do it through me. That's kind of the point to faith, right?

For an extroverted man, he may have to work to keep quiet and listen or to not be so aggressive. Same result—different perspective.

I have a friend who is a professional comedian. I actually was a fan before I became a friend, so I was surprised to find out he is really an introvert. He is basically shy and quiet. I never would have thought that about him. But you put him on stage with a mike and he becomes a redeemed Robin Williams! It's an amazing transformation. It is the power of God.

Question time again—Have you told God "no" to something because it didn't "fit" your personality? Do you ever remind Him of your personality type and why the assignment He is attempting to give you just won't work because of how He made you? (Yes, I have done this too. That's how I know the question.)

When it comes to being involved in your church's ministry, we have to be really careful, because many churches give out positions based on personality, not spiritual gifting. This is harmful because it operates only on the appearance of what someone could be good at. We can say 'yes' to something the church asks us to do, just because it fits our personality, but it doesn't mean that God has gifted us or desires us to do it.

Here's some common scenarios: "He's just so good with people. He needs to be teaching Sunday school." Someone who is "good" with people isn't necessarily a teacher of Scripture. Or "He wants to be in the Easter musical, but we'll let him help backstage. He's too quiet to be given a character role." These are just examples, but they happen everyday. All this does is keep people in their boxes, while God is about challenging us out of our boxes and into relying on Him! My point is not to knock churches, but to give you more evidence of how you must discern how you are viewed and how to deal with that. This is ultimately your responsibility as a believer.

## LIE DETECTOR

So, if our goal is to *Speak True,* then how do we become men of truth?

*Jesus said, "If you hold to my teaching, you are really my disciples. Then you will know the truth, and the truth will set you free."*
—*John 8:31b–32 NIV*

We can find at least three things here in Jesus' statement regarding truth:

1. He doesn't just know truth. He isn't a path to truth. He IS Truth! Want to know the qualities of truth? Study the life of Jesus. He is the Rock from which all Truth flows.

2. Being Truth, He is the absence of lies. Scripture calls Satan the father of lies. Where Jesus is, the Truth resides, therefore where no lies can exist. As His truth penetrates us, the enemy's lies dissipate from us.

> AS GOD'S TRUTH PENETRATES US, THE ENEMY'S LIES DISSIPATE FROM US.

3. We will find Truth by no other means, except through Christ. Searching inside ourselves, the ways of the world, or through the many belief systems of the ages won't produce Truth. Only Christ. And it is amazing how many of the world's truths that are correct are just borrowed principles from Scripture. Because that's where Truth began.

So, you may say, *"That sounds real spiritual, Robert, but how do I integrate this truth into my life?"* As you develop a personal relationship with Christ, you are actually spending time with the Truth. Prayer. Listening. Reading His Word. Solid teaching. Spending time with brothers who love Him. We all know you become whom you hang out with. Players tend to play at the level of their coaching. The more you spend time with Christ, the more you allow Him access into your thoughts, attitudes, motives, words, and actions, then the more Truth you allow in, the more Truth becomes a part of who you are. By Him. Through Him. Because of Him. To break it down, spend time with liars, learn to lie. Spend time with Truth, learn truth.

Here's some practical helps:

**To become a man of Truth, you must:**

**Get rid of the lies you tell yourself.**

In my years of discipling men, it's been challenging to help each one discover and uncover their lies, because we all have them. It's just a matter of how many and how severe they are. But for us all, the lies can be roadblocks to achieving any real growth in life.

These lies may have been said to you from someone in your past or ones you have come to believe about yourself with no one's help. They may have been said once or repeated over and over for years. Someone else may have been the original source, but now you are the source. The point is you keep repeating the lies each day and it must stop.

Obviously, the first step is to recognize them. They can become such a part of you that you convince yourself they are true, so it is hard for you to see them as lies. Like the old high school or college buddy who always got you into trouble, but you could just never seem to tell him to take a hike—that's what these lies may have become for you. Comfortable, but catastrophic.

Lies such as:

| | |
|---|---|
| I'm no good. | I'm stupid. |
| I won't ever amount to anything. | I'm ugly. |
| I'm not as good as everyone else. | I can't be forgiven. |
| I can't be loved. | What I feel doesn't matter. |
| My sin is unforgiveable. | God won't bless me. |

Take a second and circle any of these lies that you believe about yourself.

Now that you get this concept, next, I want you to take a few minutes, and in the space provided below, write down any other lies that you tell yourself.

_____

_____

_____

_____

_____

A major source of the condemnation, judgment, accusations, and lies that run through our hearts and minds come from the enemy of God. His rock gushes so much it can drown us!

I once heard James Robison, the renowned preacher, president of *Life Outreach International*, and host of *Life Today*, address this topic. He shared that even after decades of preaching and teaching to millions of people, even today while speaking, he still regularly hears things like: "You talk too long." "They aren't listening to you." "You're putting people to sleep." "You aren't as good of a speaker as their pastor." Most people would think all Robison would feel is confidence when he stood up to speak, but the decades in ministry to millions of people haven't silenced the enemy. Unfortunately, anyone who teaches, testifies, or speaks of Jesus will likely hear this same voice.

*Then I heard a loud voice in heaven say: "Now have come the salvation and the power and the kingdom of our God, and the authority of his Christ. For the accuser of our brothers, who accuses them before our God day and night, has been hurled down. They overcame him by the blood of the Lamb and by the word of their testimony. —Revelation 12:10–11a NIV*

Satan is called what? … The accuser. Accuser of who? … The brothers. Who are the brothers? … Mankind. Us, gentlemen. You and me. And what is it that he does? … Accuses, blames, makes charges against us day and night. Day and night would mean he never stops. Now, this passage also tells us his fate in the end—"hurled down." Where? "Down." How? "Hurled." By Whom? Christ. If you get hurled down, you have been officially whupped—as we say in Texas.

This passage also tells us how we can now overcome him daily. By the blood of Christ that covers our sin and the word of our testimony, which is the truth of God in our lives. Now, get this: The word of our testimony is what we speak about Christ. If I give a testimony, I am telling what Christ has done for me. The truth about Jesus overcomes the enemy's accusations. There is a lot of bad we can say about ourselves and it would be true, but we are no longer basing our lives on us and our reputation, but Christ and His! It is His blood and the truth about Him that changes us and defeats Satan. I'm going to repeat this truth. It is vitally important you understand this: We are no longer basing our lives on us and our reputation, but Christ and His! That is the only way we can *speak true*.

> WE ARE NO LONGER BASING OUR LIVES ON US AND OUR REPUTATION, BUT CHRIST AND HIS!

Regardless of the source of our lies, whether Satan, someone else, our own voice—or all three—we would love for the truth of Christ to just invade our lies, take over, and then we just supernaturally stop believing them. Miraculous healing from lies! But that's not how it works. Christ wants us to lay them down before Him and then take up His truth in their place. Christ will never break down a door, but He will walk through one when it is opened. That is when we can really begin to be men of truth.

Here's a practical way that you can replace lies using God's Word:

**Old Lie:** "You'll never amount to anything."

**New Truth:** *"So you are no longer a slave, but a son; and since you are a son, God has made you also an heir."* —Galatians 4:7 NIV

**Make it personal:** So I am no longer a slave, but a son; and since I am a son, God has made me also an heir.

**Old Lie:** "My sin is unforgiveable."

**New Truth:** *"In him we have redemption through his blood, the forgiveness of sins, in accordance with the riches of God's grace that he lavished on us with all wisdom and understanding."* — Ephesians 4:7–8 NIV

**Make it personal:** In him I have redemption through his blood, the forgiveness of sins, in accordance with the riches of God's grace that he lavished on me with all wisdom and understanding.

Find a truth in Scripture that refutes and replaces your lie. Write it down. Put it in your car. Put it on the fridge. Write it with your wife's lipstick on the bathroom mirror. (If you're single, use a Sharpie.) Get

the new truth in front of you. You worked very hard to teach yourself
the lies. Now work just as hard to take in the new truth.

The three steps to ridding yourself of lies and embracing truth are:

1.  **Refute**
    Deny their power over you and pronounce them as false.

2.  **Repent**
    Turn away from the lies and toward God. Do a 180.

3.  **Replace**
    Put a truth from God in the place of the lie.

To draw from Chapter 5, you must "pull a weed" and "plant" a truth.

Jesus used Scripture to combat the enemy, so the best way for us
to stop the enemy's lies is also with God's Word. Look at these excerpts
from Matthew 4:1–11 NIV.

*The tempter came to him and said, "If you are the Son of God, tell
these stones to become bread." Jesus answered, "It is written: 'Man does
not live on bread alone, but on every word that comes from the mouth of
God.'" [ref. Deuteronomy 8:3]*

*Then the devil took him to the holy city and had him stand on the
highest point of the temple. "If you are the Son of God," he said, "throw
yourself down. Jesus answered him, "It is also written: 'Do not put the
Lord your God to the test.'" [ref. Deuteronomy 6:16]*

*Again, the devil took him to a very high mountain and showed him
all the kingdoms of the world and their splendor. "All this I will give you,"
he said, "if you will bow down and worship me." Jesus said to him, "Away
from me, Satan! For it is written: 'Worship the Lord your God, and serve
him only.'" [ref. Deuteronomy 6:13]*

*Then the devil left him …*

**To become a man of Truth, you must:**
**Get rid of the lies you tell to others.**

**Lies**

False statements. Untruths. Deceptions. ... You get it.

**Embellishments**

Making the story sound better than it was or is. Expanding on the truth using lies. Taking the truth and adding lies to it.

*Example:*

Embellished story: "Yeah, I got up in this guy's face and told him to not ever say anything like that to me again and he backed down."

Actual story: "Uh, hey man, that wasn't cool," as you walk away.

For guys, embellishments are usually what we wish we would have done or said or what the outcome would have been, which is different from what actually happened or what we actually said.

**Half-truths**

Telling enough of the story to get some truth told, but leaving other parts out to avoid the whole truth, especially the part of the story that implicates us. If you have only a half-truth, then the other half has to be a lie.

*Example:*

Half-truth: "I know I'm 30 minutes late, but the traffic was horrible."

Truth: Traffic was slow, but you left work 15 minutes after you were supposed to.

**Patronizations**

Telling people what you believe they want to hear just to appease or manipulate the situation. We normally use patronizations to get our way or deflect the blame from us.

*Example:*

Patronization: "I really want you to partner with me on this project, because you are just so creative with awesome ideas."

Truth: I'm behind on my deadline and don't have a clue how I can finish without help.

When a man struggles with one or more of these areas, it tends to get worse over time. If a man embellishes stories with the same crowd, then the stories have to get bigger and better to get the same reaction. If a man learns to patronize his family or his co-workers, the manipulation has to get stronger over time to keep the same effect.

Lies, embellishments, half-truths, and patronizations can all become addictions in a man's speech.

*The Lord detests lying lips, but He delights in men who are truthful.*
—*Proverbs 12:22* NIV

In my first year of ministry around 1980, I helped out as a volunteer in the youth ministry of the church where I was a member. There was a teenager who came to everything the church had. He was from a bad home situation and preferred to be with us more than anywhere else. He never did well at school, so church was his safe haven. He was a great kid who you just couldn't help but like. One problem though. A big problem. He couldn't tell you the truth to save his life. He was a pathological liar. No matter how much we talked to him, prayed with him, called him on the carpet about lying, and no matter how much he apologized and said he would never do it again, one thing you could count on—he would lie to you again tomorrow. I'm talking, if he said he went to Burger King for lunch, he probably went to McDonald's. Even lying about things that didn't matter.

This young man eventually graduated from high school and decided to join the Navy. We told him goodbye and vowed to stay in touch. We were all praying that somehow the Armed Forces could help him mature and get help.

Several months later, I was in a very public place amongst several hundred people and a man walks up to me in a suit with a big clipboard. He flashes his badge and credentials and says he is with the

United States government and has a few questions for me. Well, I can tell you that in that moment my life flashed before my eyes. Traffic tickets. Tax returns. Tags ripped from pillows. Everything I had ever done flew through my cerebral cortex. I became afraid. Very afraid.

But his next words stunned me. His visit wasn't about me. He was on official business about the young pathological liar. It seems after basic training and testing, one of the potential jobs he was offered from Uncle Sam was handling top-secret information. I remember the questions like it was yesterday.

"Would you trust this man to be in the possession of highly classified information of the U.S. government?" I answered, "Absolutely not." He continued, "Do you believe this man could handle carrying the secrets of the U.S. Navy?" Again, I answered, "Absolutely not." The guy never flinched. He just kept asking questions. The longer it went, the worse I felt. But what was I to do? The knowledge I had of this young man could literally affect the security of our nation.

When he was finished with his questions, I said, "Sir, I am very sorry to have to shoot this guy down, but for the time I have known him, he has had a serious issue with lying." The agent replied, "Yeah, I know. That's what I've gotten from everyone he put down as a reference."

The very sad truth was this young man's future was not going to turn out like he had hoped, because he left a past full of lies and could never be honest in his present. Our lies, embellishments, half-truths, and patronizations can harm us in the same manner.

(Side note: I then asked the government agent, "I'm here among hundreds of people. How in the world did you find me in this crowd with no picture? He smiled and said, "Your friends described you very well." … I was amazed by his trained skill, as I stood there in my purple parachute pants and high-top Reeboks … early '80s, okay?)

**To become a man of Truth, you must:**
**Rid yourself of unforgiveness.**

Too many men are derailed for many years because they refuse to forgive someone and then a list begins to grow. When we start holding people hostage inside our bitterness, tied to the chair of their offense towards us, it becomes much easier to take more hostages. The first one makes the next ones even easier. You've already set up shop for taking hostages. Your hideout where you keep your hostages is your heart. Most people will never know that you are keeping someone locked up in there. Sometimes not even the person you are holding hostage.

But here's the horrible plot twist. Whoever you won't forgive isn't really the one tied up in the chair. They aren't really your hostages. You're the hostage. You're the one bound up. Your "offender" is out walking the streets in total freedom, rarely thinking about you. But he/she is on your mind daily. You are your own victim. See the irony?

Forgive me for stating the obvious here, but the only cure for unforgiveness is forgiveness.

As I have said on other topics, if you have no struggle in this area, that is great. Then use this information in two ways: first, keep it for yourself to keep your heart and mind swept clean. And, second, use this info and the tools coming up in Chapter 11 to minister to people in these areas. That is part of being Christ's ambassador of reconciliation (2 Corinthians 5:20). We help people make things right through Him. But, if you are struggling with unforgiveness, keep reading. Chapter 11 goes deeper into this issue, offering practical help and understanding to experiencing freedom and becoming a man of truth.

The bottom line is: Forgiveness is tough. Our culture has wanted us to believe for far too long that unforgiveness and being calloused is a man's right to be right. How many times have you seen a family divided over a man not letting go of his pride? But a real man forgives. A real man lets go. Just ask Jesus about hanging on the cross. Ask Him if forgiveness is easy. So, if we are going to follow Him, then forgiveness is not an option, but a commandment. Christ does, so we must. He has, so we should. He says to, so we do. It really should be that cut-and-dried. Now, let's go deeper …

## Discussion Questions

1.  Can you relate to John Mayer's lyrics? Any "Stupid Mouth" stories you want to share?

2.  How are our words a gauge of our purity? Why are our words a gauge of our purity?

3.  Tell whether you are an extrovert or introvert and why you know you are that personality type. Give examples. What positives do you see with your personality type? What negatives?

4.  How does it help us as Christ's followers that He is Truth and not just a path to truth?

5.  Share at least one lie that you tell yourself and why you think you believe it. (List on p. 125)

6.  Why do you think Satan would want to focus much of his time on accusing us? What would that get him?

7.  Discuss the "Refute, Repent, Replace" concept on page 128. How do you think renouncing a lie and replacing it with Scripture could help you?

8.  Which one of these do you or have you struggled with the most: lies, embellishments, half-truths, or patronizations? Why do you think that has been an issue for you? How are you fighting/working on that?

9.  Discuss the hostage concept on page 132.

10. Why would unforgiveness not have a place in a man of truth? What are some reasons we struggle with letting go of something?

    Pray a closing prayer in your own words.

CHAPTER 11

# SPEAK TRUE
# TRUTH FROM THE INSIDE OUT

*"You better put it all behind you 'cause life goes on*
*If you keep carryin' that anger, it'll eat you up inside*
*I've been tryin' to get down to the heart of the matter*
*But my will gets weak and my thoughts seem to scatter*
*But I think it's about ... forgiveness"* [1]
*—Don Henley*

"Man, he's got a temper on him, doesn't he?" Has somebody ever said that about you? You ever said that about a buddy? A family member? A co-worker? It can be said of us when we're two or sixty-two. Funny how temper has nothing to do with age, background, race, size, income, or any of the things we might see as dividing lines among men. Anger is an issue most all of us as men have to deal with at some point, on some level.

Most unforgiveness in men begins with anger. Hurt may have started the issue, but anger can quickly begin to overshadow. This is most definitely a hot-button issue for guys. In this chapter, we're going to begin by taking apart one of Paul's most well-known and practical passages to get some insight on truth and dealing with anger.

## ANGER MANAGEMENT

*"And do not grieve the Holy Spirit of God, with whom you were sealed for the day of redemption. Get rid of all bitterness, rage and an-*

*ger, brawling and slander, along with every form of malice. Be kind and compassionate to one another, forgiving each other, just as in Christ God forgave you."* —Ephesians 4:30–32 NIV

Most every Bible translation of verse 30 uses the word "grieve." When God's Spirit has sacrificed everything to forgive us for all our sin and then we choose not to forgive, it is compared to when someone we love dies. Grief. It brings great sadness and sorrow to the Lord, because we choose death over life.

Let's take a look at the first three vices that Paul tells the Ephesians to "get rid of" in verse 31. And these are all pertinent issues for us today.

### Bitterness

The Greek word this is translated from suggests a root that produces the fruit of hatred. As a bitter fruit will produce a bad taste in your mouth, hatred produces a bitter quality in your life. This is the same concept we discussed in Chapter 5 with the weeds and their roots. Anger is the root that, when not pulled out, eventually produces bitterness, and in full bloom, becomes hatred.

### Rage

This means sudden outbursts and threats that are fueled by anger. When someone "flies into a rage," we always know that anger is the source of the behavior and anger is now controlling the person. It is the picture of a lit fuse on a bomb. Anger-sssssssssssssssssssss-Rage! Rage is an emotional explosion of anger.

You can bet that if a man has a tendency toward rage, he has a constant stream of unresolved anger issues in his heart. His fuse is always lit. That's why explosions happen so quickly for him.

### Anger

*"In your anger do not sin": Do not let the sun go down while you are still angry"* —Ephesians 4:26 NIV

Here Paul talks about being angry and *not* sinning. In other words, anger is a justified emotion, when the motivation is righteousness, and the object is not focused on people, but unrighteous actions.

For me, I can honestly say that very little of my anger could be classified as righteous. As we grow closer to Christ, we have the potential to enact this concept, but being angry only for righteousness' sake is a tough one.

In the Gospels of Matthew (21:12–13), Mark (11:15–17), and John (2:14–16), each document Jesus' anger in the Temple. But he hurt no one. He attacked no one. He did turn over their tables and drive them out with a whip. He stopped their behavior. He cursed no one, but quoted Scripture about the intention of God's house. This concept teaches an angry jealousy for the glory of God, not promoting anyone's self-interests. Mylon Lefevre had a hit song years ago entitled, "Love God, Hate Sin." That's the idea here.

Now in contrast to verse 31, Paul is speaking of anger that does lead to sin. When anger is unrighteous and remains, it's like cracking open a door for Satan. A snake can't crawl in through a closed door! But give him just a small crack and he will slither in every time.

Let's look at two different progressions of anger. One is man's way and the other is God's way. Verse 26 vs. verse 31. But it is important to understand that both begin at the same place—anger.

## Self-Centered Progression of Anger

Anger
↓
Grudge
↓
Bitterness
↓
Hatred

**How can you know when anger turns to a grudge?**

When someone mentions that person's name or you think of that person and you feel angry right away, just as if the issue happened yesterday. A grudge keeps anger fresh. If someone mentions their name and you feel you have to turn on your "tape" to play about how bad they are or how much you don't like them, that's a grudge.

**How can you know when a grudge turns to bitterness?**

Oftentimes, at the grudge stage you will consider getting things straight. You are angry, but still willing to reconcile. Bitterness often causes refusal of reconciliation. That's the big difference—bitterness is when you are no longer willing or wanting to reconcile. You have taken someone hostage in your heart.

> BITTERNESS IS WHEN YOU ARE NO LONGER WILLING OR WANTING TO RECONCILE. YOU HAVE TAKEN SOMEONE HOSTAGE IN YOUR HEART.

**How can you know when bitterness turns to hatred?**

A major indicator of hatred is when you want that person completely out of your life and the cost of seeing that happen slowly becomes a lower and lower consideration. This is why for any law enforcement agency, hatred is such a strong motive for murder. Hatred can cause a very sane person to be so filled with anger that all they can think of is eliminating the person, because they finally lose the ability to consider the personal cost.

Ironically, the person that is hated loses value, but then you devalue yourself as well, because you will jeopardize your own life to take action against the person. One of the games the enemy plays here is to convince the person hating that to physically eliminate the person will actually take care of their problem and life can return to normal. Of course, that only brings devastation to everyone involved. This can also be a motivation for suicide, because self-hate overtakes all reasoning. And, unfortunately, this is the dead end that many failed marriages create.

There are times where a man is full of hatred at a number of situations in his life, but feels powerless to act with those he hates. Suddenly, in a crowded room, or an exchange with an innocent person, those feelings fly like gas through a funnel to a fire, and ignites a horrible rage. We know when we hear a story about road rage ending in a death that it was never about cutting someone off in traffic. It was unresolved and misdirected anger coming out at the wrong place at the wrong time.

If you are reading this and you know you have an anger issue, coupled with a tendency toward rage, realize that getting help now could stop a tragedy down the road. It could stop someone from getting hurt, losing a job, a spouse, children, or even getting killed. If this is you, do not wait. The enemy could be baiting your last trap right now. What if your next anger outburst is the last one your wife will put up with? What if the next situation you finally go too far with the violence?

For others of you, is there a relationship (or relationships) in your life where you're in one of the four stages—anger, grudge, bitterness, or hatred? Did looking at the progression and definitions make you realize you are deeper into anger than you realized? Is your issue with an old relationship? Is it an ex-wife? A wayward child? Estranged family member? Ex-employer? Ex-partner? Ex-friend? Who?

I promise if you find yourself consistently in the grudge stage with people or struggling with bitterness, it will affect your ability to speak truth and it will affect your purity as well. Why? Because your motives stay tainted. Your heart is haunted by constant bitterness. You're choosing death over life with no end in sight.

> IF YOU FIND YOURSELF CONSISTENTLY IN THE GRUDGE STAGE WITH PEOPLE OR STRUGGLING WITH BITTERNESS, IT WILL AFFECT YOUR ABILITY TO SPEAK TRUTH AND IT WILL AFFECT YOUR PURITY.

Wouldn't this be a great time to get things right? The perfect time to forgive or seek forgiveness? *"So, Robert, why is this the perfect time?"* Because you are dealing with it right now! It is no coincidence that you are reading this and you have been reminded and convicted of a relationship that needs to be made right.

The rest is up to you. What do you have to do? Make a phone call? Get in the car? Write an e-mail? A letter? It does not matter at all how the other person responds. God only holds you responsible for your part.

The enemy wants you to believe that letting your anger go and releasing forgiveness towards them will make the other person "win." He tells you that if you forgive, you lose. So, how's that been working for you so far? Do you really feel like you're "winning" right now?

As we stated in the last chapter, you are being held in bondage inside the house of hatred. Know that letting it go and granting forgiveness will feel awesome. You will feel like ten tons has dropped off your back. Shut the door on the enemy and release the real hostage—YOU! The other person isn't imprisoned—it's you. Let them go, so you can free yourself.

Walking through forgiveness and getting rid of bitterness and hatred are done best when you have some help. Talk to a pastor or a trusted Christian friend right away to work through the issues and get a plan. Prayer and accountability are important tools to getting well and seeking truth in your life.

Just like in the purity chapters, if none of this is your issue, you may have read this to help a brother or family member that you know is struggling. Why not talk to them about it? Why not ask them to read this chapter? A major focus of this book is when you read something that is not your issue, then use the information as training to help others. Love your neighbor as yourself.

## Not Keeping Score

*Then Peter came to Jesus and asked, "Lord, how many times shall I forgive my brother when he sins against me? Up to seven times?" Jesus answered, "I tell you, not seven times, but seventy-seven times.*
—Matthew 18:21–22 NIV

The concept of Jesus' statement is that you forgive so much that you stop counting. You know, like God does with us? (How'd you like to know that number? Okay, Robert, you are up to 1,683,927 times I have forgiven you.) Bottom line here is we must forgive others as often and as much as God forgives us. Last I looked that was an unlimited supply.

Do you see how purity is strongly connected to truth in our lives? It's a unity of concepts that must become one in our souls. One flows into the other like a good marriage.

Let's go back now to Ephesians 4:31 and focus on the phrase "get rid of." This means "every trace gone." (Our roots talk in Chapter 5.)

Did you ever make a big mess when you were a kid and your mom came in, freaked out, and said, "When I come back in here in thirty minutes, I want every trace of this mess cleaned up!" That's the idea. Except God doesn't yell like mom does and He does the clean-up.

Much like our earlier discussion of true Biblical purity, Paul is communicating that he wants the Ephesian Christians to have a total abstinence of evil. As with Jesus' definition of adultery, it's more than just *not* practicing evil, but not even *thinking* about evil, not allowing it to take root in our hearts to open the door to the enemy. (See the amazing consistency of God here?) As we get closer to Christ, we will better understand this purity progression in every area of life.

Let's look at the three commands Paul gives in verse 32.

*Be kind and compassionate to one another, forgiving each other, just as in Christ God forgave you.*

1.  **Be kind.**
    Kindness is love in practical action. How do you know someone is showing kindness? They are doing kind things. Expressing love.

2.  **Compassionate**
    Compassion in the heart is the motive for being kind and applying love in practical action. Compassion is the root and kindness is the fruit.

3.  **Forgiving**

    Whenever you make a practice of forgiveness and dealing graciously with people, then you can be consistent in feeling compassion and committing to acts of kindness.

Now, watch this. … When you take the definitions we have applied to the three vices (anger, rage, bitterness) and the three virtues (compassion, kindness, forgiveness), we find something very interesting. And Paul often practiced this in his teaching and writing.

Anger versus compassion.

Rage versus kindness.

Bitterness versus forgiveness.

Do you see how these stand in contrast to one another? Ridding ourselves of these three vices and practicing the three virtues is both defense and offense. We not only stop words and actions that hurt others and ourselves, but we can be pro-active in representing Christ and promoting His Kingdom. Then finally, we see that the reason we can live this new life is because God in Christ has forgiven us. That is what the Knight's Code is ultimately all about!

A few pages ago, we looked at self-centered anger. Here it is again:

Anger

⬇

Grudge

⬇

Bitterness

⬇

Hatred

Now, here is what happens when we give our anger to God.

Anger

⬇

Resolve

⬇

Forgiveness

⬇

Love

Both lists begin with the same emotion and response—anger. But when taken away from our flesh and given to God, things turn positive quickly. When we sin, what does God immediately desire and seek with us? Resolve. So should we with others.

Remember when we said earlier that resolve is still an option in the grudge stage? That is the key point and crossroads. If we will head toward resolve, then a grudge never occurs, so bitterness never even takes root.

I found this story buried deep in the front section of the Sunday paper years ago. Chris Carrier of Coral Gables, Florida was eight years old when a man that was angry with his father abducted him. The kidnapper burned him with cigarettes, stabbed him numerous times with an ice pick, shot him in the head, and then dumped him out to die in the Everglades. Miraculously, Chris survived and was found. His only lasting physical effect from the ordeal was losing sight in one eye. His attacker was never captured.

Carrier became a Christian, and later became a youth pastor, serving at a church in Florida. One day, he received word that a man named David McAllister, a 77-year-old frail and blind ex-con living in a Miami Beach nursing home had finally confessed to committing the crime all those years ago.

So Carrier headed to Miami. Did he take his gun? Did he plot revenge on the way there? After all, now the tables were turned. The old man was helpless, just as he was when McAllister tortured, shot, and left him for dead. … No. Revenge wasn't Chris' motive, as was his captor's. Carrier was going God's direction. Resolve and forgiveness. And, amazingly, yes, even love.

Chris began visiting McAllister regularly and often read the Bible and prayed with him. Through these visits, Carrier eventually led McAllister to his Lord. Carrier said, "While many people can't understand how I could forgive David McAllister, from my point of view, I couldn't not forgive him. If I'd chosen to hate him all these years, or spent my life looking for revenge, then I wouldn't be the man I am today, the man my wife and children love, the man God has helped me to be."[2]

To say that Chris Carrier was never angry over what had happened to him would be ridiculous, but what an awesome testimony of both receiving and giving God's grace. An amazing example of the power of giving anger to God.

## The Path of Wrath

One of the best ways for us to know how to deal with our anger is to look at when God gets angry. Because even a light read of Scripture picks up on the fact that God can get very mad, yet—obviously—without sin. We also see plenty more times that He could have been angry, yet He chose another approach. When you look at all Scripture together as a whole, here are some principles we find.

1. God's commands are always an expression of His love.

2. God's anger is always an expression of His righteousness. One of God's responses when the right(eous) thing is not done is to get angry. What is the right(eous) thing? His commands.

3. God's righteousness is an expression of His faithfulness to act on behalf of those who love Him.

He cares about us so deeply that He wants us to do the right thing and be right(eous). But as we know, being right (our way) and being righteous (His ways) are two very different concepts.

*"Time after time he restrained His anger."* —*Psalm 78:38* NIV

*"For his anger lasts only a moment, but his favor lasts a lifetime."*
                                        —*Psalm 30:4* NIV

## THAT'S HOW WE DO IT!

The final section of *Speak True* is a list of ten practical principles to help you apply truth in your life.

**1.  Make a list of people that you won't, or can't, find the strength to forgive.**

Sit down in a quiet place and talk to God about your list. Tell Him all about how you feel and why you feel the way you do. Be deadly honest. He can handle it. Next, ask Him what to do about each person on your list. Do what He tells you to do with each one. Generally, He will give you two choices. The first is to forgive the person and give your anger and that person to Him, because there are times when personal interaction is not possible or somehow not best for thc situation.

The second is to go to the person. You may need to talk over the issues. You may simply need to ask for or grant forgiveness and you don't require anything from them.

For serious and deep offenses, you may need to get accountability from a brother and/or guidance from a counselor. The bottom line here is to do as Paul commanded and "get rid of" your list of anger, grudges, bitterness, and hatred.

**2.  Once you take care of your list, then keep your list short.**

The best tactic is as Paul stated to, "not let the sun go down on your anger." Get things resolved quickly. If you or the other person need to allow time to process or cool down, that's fine, but as soon as is possible, get it straight. I once heard a Bible teacher say, "You can measure your maturity level as a Christian by the length of time between the offense and your resolve." Wouldn't it feel good to know you keep your list clean, so it never builds up again? Accountability between brothers is a great way to keep your list short.

Learn to apologize quickly—don't wait for one first. The faster you get it right, the less time there is for things to go wrong. Humble yourself. That ends the list fast.

Face to face verbal communication is always best. Calling over the phone is the second preference. E-mails, texts, etc. can lose meaning and personal touch. Avoid those unless it is the only means available.

### 3.  Develop a set of truth principles.

We defined and discussed principles in *Live Pure*. It's the same concept here, just applied to different aspects of life.

Here's some examples that cover both offense and defense.

Offense/Positive—My wife and I are out with friends and I think about how beautiful she is. I need to tell her what I thought on the way home. She needs to hear that.

Defense/negative—If I "vent" or share some issues I have with another brother to someone, then I must plan on getting things right as soon as I possibly can. It's not about getting someone "on my side" and gossip against a brother, but getting a proper plan of action to Biblically take care of my issue.

Let me just tell you if you decide to move from typical gossip to creating accountability in your statements by going directly to that person and sharing those thoughts, you will, unfortunately, create some enemies along the way. Lots of people, including some Christians, don't like people who speak truth. It seems we often prefer to just operate in the knowledge that we all gossip with no backbone. We will all spout off about someone from time to time, but what we do after that is a strong gauge of our own integrity.

> LOTS OF PEOPLE, INCLUDING SOME CHRISTIANS, DON'T LIKE PEOPLE WHO SPEAK TRUTH.

Allow me to share with you the situation that led me to this principle in my own life several years ago. A friend had recommended I begin a business dealing with someone that they worked with. I called and left messages. No response. I e-mailed. No response. So, I wrote my friend an e-mail and said how doing business like that wouldn't help this person stay in business very long, yada yada yada, gripe, gripe, gripe. Well, what did my busy, cut-to-the-chase friend do? He just hit forward on the e-mail to the person. Within a few hours, I received a phone call. When I answered the call, I wasn't sure if I would be met with anger or humility. It was humility. But I have to tell you I was the more humbled and I vowed that day that I wouldn't say anything or write an e-mail or make a phone call that I wouldn't back up and say straight to the person. If I can't, then I don't need to say or write it. In fact, I better just skip the friend and go straight to the source. This approach needs grace and tact, as well as prayer, but wouldn't our word and reputation become much stronger if we began to regularly practice this? Which brings me to number four …

**4.   Let your 'yes' be 'yes' and your 'no' be 'no.' (Matthew 5:37 & James 5:12)**

This doesn't mean you can never change your mind, but that you gain a reputation for making concise, steady, firm decisions. Be a man of your word. The current culture of men we live in today seems to be afraid to make a decision and stand on it. Then if it backfires, blame and deflection seem to be Plan B. Christian men should be counter-cultural and make firm, Biblical decisions, then take the hit if it's wrong. And be humble if it's right!

**5.   Attitude and tone are just as crucial as your words.**

This is one of my major issues and struggles. I am fairly consistent with my words, but I blow it a lot in this area. I can say the right thing the wrong way and the right thing is never heard, because *how* I said it overshadowed what I said! This comes from my being too intense. The intensity comes up and bites me. When I was young and would tell my dad that someone at school called me little, he would smile and say, "Son, tell them you're not little, you're just wound tight." Man, is that still true! And something I have to constantly lay on the altar to sacrifice.

Over the years, I have supervised a lot of employees. One time I had a young man ask me if he could take off on a certain day to help his parents move. I thought through everyone's schedule for a moment and then told him he could take off. Several days later, I realized he had been at work on that day, so I asked him what happened, and why his parents weren't able to move? He said, "No, they moved." I, now puzzled, asked, "Well, how come you didn't help?" He answered, "Well, I could just tell when I asked you if I could take off that day that you didn't really want me to be gone." When I asked him if I had said he could take off work, he said yes, but, "it wasn't what you said, it was how you said it." … I was crushed. I learned a big lesson that day and, unfortunately still learn it at least once a week. We all got our stuff and this is one of mine. Well, there you go. If this is your issue, watch your mouth. … Oh, I'm sorry, did that have a tone?

**6. Our words either ATTRACT people to Christ or DISTRACT people from Christ.**

Here's a few thoughts on the Distract side.

Rude, vulgar, crass, racial, and sexist remarks have no place in a Christian man's daily language. Yes, there are situations and certain people where a comfort level allows for an understanding of certain remarks because of a context or meaning with a select group of friends. I'm talking about allowing comments and remarks on a regular basis that would not only distract people from the God you serve, but even potentially deflect them from Him. When others have no context on us, they assume our speech is a complete reflection of our heart.

*These men are springs without water and mists driven by a storm. Blackest darkness is reserved for them. For they mouth empty, boastful words and, by appealing to the lustful desires of sinful human nature, they entice people who are just escaping from those who live in error. They promise them freedom, while they themselves are slaves of depravity—for a man is a slave to whatever has mastered him. If they have escaped the corruption of the world by knowing our Lord and Savior Jesus Christ and are again entangled in it and overcome, they are worse off at the end than they were at the beginning. —2 Peter 2:17–20 NIV*

Now, here's a few thoughts on the Attract side.

*The Lord was with Samuel as he grew up and he let none of his words fall to the ground. —1 Samuel 3:19 NIV*

Translation: Samuel gained a reputation for being reliable in what he said of the Lord.

*Let your conversation be always full of grace, seasoned with salt, so that you may know how to answer everyone. —Colossians 4:6 NIV*

Who should we be ready to answer? Everyone.
When will everyone ask or talk to you? Anytime.
So when should we be ready? Always.
Doesn't that warrant us learning to speak as Jesus would?

### 7.   Christian men are not silent men.

I said silent, not quiet. There's a difference. A lot of men don't have to worry about saying too much or too little, because you're just not going to hear from them at all! Listen, gentlemen, silence has hurt just as many people as words have. Sometimes it's not *what* you say, but what you *don't* say. I used Psalm 39:1 earlier, but now read it with verse 2.

*"I will watch my ways and keep my tongue from sin; I will put a muzzle on my mouth. But when I was silent and still, not even saying anything good, my anguish increased." —Psalm 39:1–2 NIV*

Silence, not words, produced anguish. How many of us have experienced anguish in our lives from a father that never said "I love you" or "I'm proud of you" or "that's my boy"? How many of us are repeating that same anguish by not saying what we need to say? How many times have you heard a man defend, "Well, my wife knows I love her." "My son knows I love him. They know men don't like to say it a lot."

Here is what silence from men always boils down to: Pride. I've always thought it was ironic that the English word "pride" has a big ol' "I" in the middle of it. If a man is sitting back being quiet when it is time to speak, it is either pride or fear keeping him quiet. And very often fear is based on not looking bad, which is just disguised pride. So, yeah, pride.

If that is you and your lack of words are hurting your wife, kids, family, co-workers, and on and on, it is time to surrender your pride, give your mouth to Christ, and your heart to the people who need to hear it.

### 8.  You provoke your own response.

*A gentle answer turns away wrath, but a harsh word stirs up anger.* —*Proverbs 15:1* NIV

How we speak is very often how we are spoken back to. Ever had a day where you keep thinking, "Why is everybody being such a jerk?" Or this: "All I did was ask a simple question and I got my head bit off?!" Hmmmm. The next simple question is how did you ask that simple question? This principle is especially true inside our families.

### 9.  Be an encourager.

The grown man who still constantly uses junior high sarcasm and cut-downs is never a popular guy. He won't get calls from friends when they are down, because they know they'll likely get kicked! If you have been employed on the Demolition Crew for too long—then just quit. The benefits are lousy anyway.

Join the Construction Crew and begin building people up. They'll feel better. You'll feel better. You'll be a better person, husband, father, and friend.

Use your words for building bridges—not burning them.

A man who freely encourages others is a rarity today. Be a rarity and God will bless you for it.

**10. Be an active listener.**

Concentrate on what the other person is saying—not on what you're going to say next.

Try to understand where the other person is coming from—not on how to get them to see your point.

Ask for clarification on what you don't understand—ask questions or recap your perspective of what you heard. This is to insure the other person that you understood them.

Take initiative in reaching the truth—be pro-active in communication. A major part of that is the art of listening.

## The Whole Truth and Nothing but the Truth, so Help Me, God

In closing the *Speak True* chapters, let's look at another of Paul's passages.

*Then we will no longer be infants, tossed back and forth by the waves, and blown here and there by every wind of teaching and by the cunning and craftiness of men in their deceitful scheming. Instead, speaking the truth in love, we will in all things grow up into him who is the Head, that is Christ. —Ephesians 4:14–15* NIV

The Message expresses verse 15 as *"to know the whole truth and tell it in love—like Christ in everything."*

By speaking the truth in love, we grow up in Him.

One way to translate the phrase "speaking the truth in love" is "truthing in love." This means a continually current mindset of mixing truth with love, love with truth. The concept is based in integrity where your beliefs match your actions. Actions match belief. Your life is truth. Your life is love. What you say, you do. What you do, you say.

We're funny, we sinner people, aren't we? We tend to either get the truth part or the love part. Often that goes back to our personalities and backgrounds. We tend to be either too aggressive or too passive. Too law or too grace.

The truth is that love is sometimes a hug and sometimes it's a swift kick in the pants. As brothers in Christ, we have to be able to give each other both and know when we need what!

The balance once again is found in the life of Christ. He was known for boldly proclaiming truth, but He was also known for boldly loving people. And He was killed on a cross for doing both. His love drove His truth and His truth drove His love. Gentlemen, we must become known for the same. That is our hope and goal. His life in us.

To end, I want to leave you with some questions to consider.

If you gave total control of your mouth to Christ right now …

… who would be apologized to that wasn't before?

… what relationship would be made right?

… who would be thanked that never had before?

… who would be told they are loved that hadn't before?

… who would be encouraged that either was discouraged before or left to silence?

… who would see—and hear—Christ in you like never before?

Let's pray.

*Father God, our Lord and King. It is both an honor and a comfort to know that You are the perfect balance of Truth and Love, because You are Truth and Love. Please teach me Your Truth. Teach me to be a man of Truth. Please teach me to love like You love. I give you my mouth, God, both to tame and to teach. May I grow in the maturity to use it for Your glory, to build others up, and to share Who You are. May I speak when You ask me to and hold my tongue when You need me to. Give me the wisdom to balance the truth I speak with the love I share. May I be a man You can count on to be Your mouthpiece in any situation, because my heart is fully Yours. Amen.*

> *What you're after is truth from the inside out.*
> *Enter me, then; conceive a new, true life.*
> *—Psalm 51:6 MSG*

## DISCUSSION QUESTIONS

1.   Share how anger affects your life. Daily battle? Occasional struggle? Relational obstacle? Train wreck?

2.   Why do you think most guys respond to being hurt by getting angry?

3.   Describe a time that you were bitter toward someone and how you dealt with it.

4.   Why do you think there is a connection between unresolved anger and rage?

5.   Do you think it's even possible to be angry about something and not sin? Why or why not?

6.   Discuss the concept of the "self-centered progression of anger" on Page 141.

7.   Discuss the concept of the "God-centered progression of anger" on Page 142.

8.   What do you think is the key to turning anger in the direction that God would have us?

9.   Share the one principle of the ten practical principles under the heading "That's How We Do It!"on Pages 144–150 that you struggle with the most or that hit home with you.

10.  Discuss the six questions on Page 151 under the text, "If you gave total control of your mouth to Christ right now …"

Close in prayer.

CHAPTER 12

# *RIGHT WRONG*
# BEWARE THE ME MONSTER

*"There's something missing from my life.*
*Cuts me open like a knife. It leaves me vulnerable.*
*I have this disease. I shake like an incurable.*
*God, help me please. There's a hole in my life."* [1]
—*Sting*

What if you walked into most any church next Sunday and asked the average man this question: Who is more committed to their tribe for life—the average Marine or the average Christian man? … There's a strong chance, unless the pastor or priest is within earshot, the answer you'll get is "the Marine." The reason? The tribe we call Marine in this nation is one of the most respected, noble, and honoring positions a man can hold—and it should be. A Marine is a Marine forever and everyone knows that. Why do we know that? Well, have you ever known a Marine? That's how we know that!

But what if years ago, the Marines had begun to have internal strife and unresolved issues about what a Marine truly is, which parts of the Handbook are crucial and which aren't, which Marine assignments were important and which weren't, and even how to properly interpret the phrase *Semper Fidelis*. So, the best option anyone could come up with to satisfy the dilemma was to divide the Marines into splinter groups according to belief on the minor issues. Sides started to form according to where they stood on procedures and protocols. It wasn't long before those groups started to disagree and more splinters developed. Why? Because the precedent had been set that when you disagree, you don't resolve, you divide. It was no longer just about being a Marine, but defining what type of Marine. You had to choose a flavor—just the brand itself was no longer enough. Now, let me ask you. Had that actually happened 100 years ago or 50 years ago, what would *Semper Fi* mean to anyone today? How would the Marines be viewed right now? How many young men would want to sign up for that movement? How many lifers would that create?

There is a bottom line brotherhood that makes the Marines, the Marines. Is it possible for us as Christian brothers to get to that same place again? What if we asked God, "Hey, God, would you like for us all to agree that You are Lord and that the Bible is Your Word? Lord, do you think You could get more done with us if we focused on the majors and let go of the minors, for the sake of unity?" What do you think He would say? And what if we actually began to do this? Would the enemy have to change strategy? … Here's the answer.

*My prayer is not that you take them out of the world but that you protect them from the evil one. They are not of the world, even as I am not of it. Sanctify them by the truth; your word is truth. As you sent me into the world, I have sent them into the world. For them I sanctify myself, that they too may be truly sanctified. My prayer is not for them alone. I pray also for those who will believe in me through their message, that all of them may be one, Father, just as you are in me and I am in you. May they also be in us so that the world may believe that you have sent me. I have given them the glory that you gave me, that they may be one as we are one: I in them and you in me. May they be brought to complete unity to let the world know that you sent me and have loved them even as you have loved me. —Jesus' prayer to the Father in John 17:15–23 NIV*

*Complete unity.* … What a great phrase.

When two Marines meet today, there is a foundational under-standing between them. It doesn't matter who served when, or for how long, or where they were stationed, or what specific job they did, it's about being a Marine. Period.

The military draft ended in 1973.[2] Since then no one is required to go into the Armed Forces. Yet everyone in this nation has always known how difficult it is to become a Marine. Everyone has heard about the horrors of boot camp and the infamous role of the drill ser-geant. Isn't it interesting that young men still sign up every day? Older men still re-up every year. There is an untainted simplicity and au-thentic identity attached forever to the title and role of "The Marine."

What can we learn from this? If Christian brotherhood ever re-turned to this same premise, how many more men would walk into church next Sunday? How many more men would be open to discuss-ing faith with us, instead of backing out the door? How many men of other belief systems would show up at the church's door?

And by the way, *Semper Fidelis* means "Always faithful."[3] I re-peat—untainted simplicity and authentic identity.

This is exactly why I have been intentional in this book to avoid introducing inspiring spiritual concepts (which for a guy can be as frustrating as trying to grab Jello), but rather introduce gut-level faith principles. I am intentionally avoiding theological splinter points and sticking with the major sin issues that plague all men.

## DEBATES & DIFFERENCES

So, you want to read only the King James? Great. You want to speak in tongues? Go for it. You don't want to speak in tongues? Don't go for it. You want to worship with a choir and pipe organ? Awesome. You want to worship with an acoustic guitar and a set of congas? Cool. No music at all, just voices? Then sing. Exegetical? Topical? Seeker-driven? Traditional? Contemporary? Could I go on and on for this en-tire chapter pointing out all the little nuances that separate us? … Yep.

Am I saying there should be no deal breakers? Absolutely not. But the deal breakers should be direct violations of Scripture. So, that said: For us to right the wrongs of our lives as brothers, we are going to have to stop focusing on the many flavors and schools of thought, and just stand under the banner of Jesus. The brand of Christ. Period. But what would change in our world if we decided we were going to simplify and *Semper Fi* to agree that Jesus is Lord and that is the only hill we will all die on?!

In the '80s and early '90s, I toured with a Christian music group. I had long hair (an awesome mullet) and played the drums, so I was already suspect in most conservative circles. (Remember that little detail.) We were invited to play at a youth camp for an after-the-service concert. It was a highly conservative, fundamentally run camp. The youth pastors that booked us knew we would win over the kids with the music (Not Stryper, more Michael W.), but then be faithful to clearly present the Gospel and give an opportunity to respond. Out of 1500 kids there, a lot of them had invited their non-Christian friends and were ready for us to tell them about Jesus in a relevant way.

In the middle of our fourth song, the camp director stormed onto the stage, grabbed the mike out of the lead singer's stand and screamed, "You kids go back to your cabins and you boys pack up your gear and go home!" … It was a very surreal moment. Didn't see that one coming, but really not surprised.

We were then asked by the youth pastors—who were now freaking out—to go into a room behind the tabernacle with them and the camp director and his assistant. We began to hear about the evils of the drumbeat and how God can never use anything but hymns. One of our guys began to tactfully explain that Jesus used various methods to reach the culture of his day and that is what we were doing. Me, being just the drummer and all, sat there and watched the back and forth of the well-thought out points of both "sides." But I saw this could go on all night and no one was going to change anyone's mind. That was when I did the unthinkable. The long-haired, evil-beat drummer spoke up. (Think Animal from *The Muppets.* That's probably close to how I was viewed by these guys.) I said, "Gentlemen, I don't think we are going to convince each other of our different methods and styles, so I'd like to ask a question to see if ultimately we stand on the same ground. Do we all agree that Jesus Christ is our Lord and Savior and that He is the Way, the Truth, and the Life and that salvation can be found in no one else? … Awkward silence. … Hushed "yes's" from all around the room. One of the youth pastors took the cue and led a closing prayer. Then we packed up our gear and went home, as we were asked. Debate officially over, calling it a draw.

Sometimes I think there are hundreds of thousands of us sitting around in a room behind the sanctuary trying to prove why we are right and others are wrong, when we need to simply agree on Jesus and get after showing the world Who He is through our lives. That is exactly why a number of years ago, I stopped debating anyone on any theological issue, but especially non-Christians. If that's your thing, I'm not criticizing you, but consider this. Have you ever heard a guy's testimony that went like this, "Well, we were in a heated argument about the legitimacy of the virgin birth and suddenly, I realized, 'Ya know, this guy is so spiritual and so articulate in his presentation that I must concede now and accept his Jesus. So I prayed right then.'"

All the testimonies I've ever heard usually have something to do with love, grace, and forgiveness, not debates and differences. Don't get sucked into trying to prove you're smarter than someone else, that's just pride.

*We know that we have passed from death to life, because we love our brothers. … This is how we know what love is: Jesus Christ laid down his life for us. And we ought to lay down our lives for our brothers. … Dear children, let us not love with words or tongue but with actions and in truth. —1 John 3:14a, 16, 18 NIV*

God's specialty is taking an ordinary man destined to commit sin and go to Hell and turning him into a warrior committed to His cause, living the abundant life, and ready to go to his home in Heaven one day when the mission is completed. Taking a condemned man with countless wrongs to be righted and turning him into an agent of change who is battling injustice on a daily basis—starting with his own and working outward to the world.

> GOD'S SPECIALTY IS TAKING AN ORDINARY MAN DESTINED TO COMMIT SIN AND GO TO HELL AND TURNING HIM INTO A WARRIOR COMMITTED TO HIS CAUSE.

*He has showed you, O man, what is good. And what does the* LORD *require of you? To act justly and to love mercy and to walk humbly with your God. —Micah 6:8* NIV

That's exactly where we're going in the next two chapters.

## A DARK KNIGHT

I want to ask you a question that I ask every men's group anytime I teach the *Right Wrong* tenet. This question is a little easier and a lot more fun to answer than many of the others we have broached. Here we go: Who is your favorite super hero?

And the follow-up question is why is that super hero your favorite?

Anytime I ask this question in any group of men, a very large percentage answer with "Batman." The answer as to why is always very much the same too. Batman has no super powers. He can't fly. He's not faster than a locomotive. He doesn't have super-human strength. But Batman is just so cool. But here's why a lot of men, including myself, like and relate to Batman. He had a tormented childhood that led to a dysfunctional adult life with no lasting relationships, except his butler who's on the payroll. Now that is really sad, isn't it? We actually feel a little sorry for him. When do we ever feel sorry for Superman? We can relate to Batman, not so much Superman.

Now here's the upside for Batman: He has an apparent unlimited amount of money, because he owns a global mega-corporation, so he's rich and powerful. Did I mention genius-level intelligence? Then throw in an alter ego that fights crime and administers justice—anonymously. What's not to love about that? Now, here's why I personally connect with Batman. He is an ordinary guy who has a driven passion to right wrong, but he has far more success righting wrong all over Gotham City than he does in his own heart. Sound familiar, gentlemen? I'm not rich. I'm not powerful. Smart, maybe, not intelligent. But I can so relate to this dilemma. Conquer the city, but fail in his own heart. As guys, we can rescue a situation in a half hour for someone else, but can't get a handle on a dysfunction of our own for a decade. I say this, because that is me. You relate? As the comic strip character *Pogo* used to say, "We have met the enemy and he is us!"[4]

## FLAWS & FAITH

Our Christian heritage is rich in heroes. Normal men who put all their trust in an Almighty God. No super powers, but an All-Powerful God. Throughout the Bible and throughout the ages, we know the names of men who lived and died by their faith in Him. One great example of a flawed, but faith-filled man is David. Whether you have studied David or you've only heard of him, let's take a look at some key events in his life.

*[Goliath] looked David over and saw that he was only a boy, ruddy and handsome, and he despised him. He said to David, "Am I a dog, that you come at me with sticks?" And the Philistine cursed David by his gods. "Come here," he said, "and I'll give your flesh to the birds of the air and the beasts of the field!" David said to the Philistine, "You come against me with sword and spear and javelin, but I come against you in the name of the LORD Almighty, the God of the armies of Israel, whom you have defied. This day the LORD will hand you over to me, and I'll strike you down and cut off your head. Today I will give the carcasses of the Philistine army to*

*the birds of the air and the beasts of the earth, and the whole world will know that there is a God in Israel. All those gathered here will know that it is not by sword or spear that the LORD saves; for the battle is the LORD's, and he will give all of you into our hands." As the Philistine moved closer to attack him, David ran quickly toward the battle line to meet him. Reaching into his bag and taking out a stone, he slung it and struck the Philistine on the forehead. The stone sank into his forehead, and he fell facedown on the ground. So David triumphed over the Philistine with a sling and a stone; without a sword in his hand he struck down the Philistine and killed him. David ran and stood over him. He took hold of the Philistine's sword and drew it from the scabbard. After he killed him, he cut off his head with the sword. —1 Samuel 17:42–51a NIV*

What an awesome "guy moment!" The last one in the bunch anyone would imagine to do anything about this and he ends up cutting the giant's head off! David saved Israel and his life took a powerful, dramatic turn. But check out another turn a few years later.

*In the spring, at the time when kings go off to war, David sent Joab out with the king's men and the whole Israelite army. They destroyed the Ammonites and besieged Rabbah. But David remained in Jerusalem. One evening David got up from his bed and walked around on the roof of the palace. From the roof he saw a woman bathing. The woman was very beautiful, and David sent someone to find out about her. The man said, "Isn't this Bathsheba, the daughter of Eliam and the wife of Uriah the Hittite?" Then David sent messengers to get her. She came to him, and he slept with her. (She had purified herself from her uncleanness.) Then she went back home. The woman conceived and sent word to David, saying, "I am pregnant." —2 Samuel 11:1–5 NIV*

Same guy, gentlemen. Yes, there were a few years in between these occurrences, but yet another example of how we can right the wrongs of a nation, yet fail in our own hearts. And it only got worse. David had her husband killed by moving him up to the battlefront (verses 14–17).

Now look closely at this:

*Create in me a pure heart, O God, and renew a steadfast spirit within me. Do not cast me from your presence or take your Holy Spirit from me. Restore to me the joy of your salvation and grant me a willing spirit, to sustain me. Then I will teach transgressors your ways, and sinners will turn back to you. Save me from bloodguilt, O God, the God who saves me, and my tongue will sing of your righteousness. —Psalm 51:10–14 NIV*

Yet again, same guy. But now broken, confessing, changing. Inside these five simple verses, men, is the key to righting the wrongs in our own hearts. Inviting God in to do what only He can do, when we have seen the worst of what we can do. Understanding that we cannot, yet He can. Believing that He wants and will use us to right wrongs in the world in spite of ourselves, once we understand that the only path to personal righteousness is in and through Him. He has to work *on* us, then *in* us, before He can work *through* us.

Look at the action words in these verses: "Create," "renew," "restore," "grant," "sustain," and "save." As the wrongs are made right, then action flows from David: "I will teach," "sinners will turn," and "my tongue will sing." This is what happens when a loving, merciful, persistent, grace-filled God intervenes in the life of a dysfunctional, issue-ridden, self-centered man. Redemption, forgiveness, salvation, and restoration occur. Righteousness meets rebellion and wrongs are made right.

In our world today, where is The Joker, or The Penguin, or Two Face, or even Goliath? The enemies don't seem to be so clearly marked in our battle. Or are they?

In the next two chapters, we'll look at all the key relationships of our lives, beginning with ourselves, which is exactly the order God works in.

## THE DRAGON TO SLAY IN OUR OWN FLESH

"I'm so embarassed that I never suspected—not a one," Elin Nordegren, Tiger Woods' ex-wife, said in her first interview since her husband's scandal broke. "For the last 3 1/2 years, when all this was going on, I was home a lot more with pregnancies, then the children and my school. I felt stupid as more things were revealed. How could I not have known anything? The word 'betrayal' isn't strong enough."[5]

Prior to his wedding in 2004, Tiger's lawyers had Elin sign a prenuptial agreement stating she could receive only $20 million should a divorce occur, only after at least ten years of marriage.[6] This was, of course, an effort to protect the world-renowned athlete's fortune, endorsements, and golden name from a woman with bad intentions.

Fast forward 5 years—following mistress after mistress coming forward to tell of his affairs with them, the tarnishing of his brand began and the divorce cost Mr. Woods an estimated $100 million.[7] Unfortunately, Tiger's lawyers and pre-nup, designed to shield him from his wife, couldn't protect him from himself.

This story tells the tale of how we often are so thorough in judging other's motives and guarding our own interests, while missing the fact that we have major issues in our own hearts that are far more threatening.

*It is obvious what kind of life develops out of trying to get your own way all the time: repetitive, loveless, cheap sex; a stinking accumulation of mental and emotional garbage; frenzied and joyless grabs for happiness; trinket gods; magic-show religion; paranoid loneliness; cutthroat competition; all-consuming-yet-never-satisfied wants; a brutal temper; an impotence to love or be loved; divided homes and divided lives; small-minded and lopsided pursuits; the vicious habit of depersonalizing everyone into a rival; uncontrolled and uncontrollable addictions; ugly parodies of community. I could go on.*

*This isn't the first time I have warned you, you know. If you use your freedom this way, you will not inherit God's kingdom.*

*But what happens when we live God's way? He brings gifts into our lives, much the same way that fruit appears in an orchard—things like affection for others, exuberance about life, serenity. We develop a willingness to stick with things, a sense of compassion in the heart, and a conviction that a basic holiness permeates things and people. We find ourselves*

*involved in loyal commitments, not needing to force our way in life, able*
*to marshal and direct our energies wisely. —Galatians 5:19–23* MSG

Paul clearly outlines the life we can live in our own flesh versus the life we may live inside the Kingdom of God. This battle will be fought our entire lives. But we can't talk seriously about righting wrong anywhere until we have first focused on living pure and speaking truth. Purity and truth are foundational concepts to any belief system, but particularly in Christianity. Think about it, if my life is full of lust and lies, then why would I care about righting anyone's wrongs? In fact, very often, that lifestyle encourages others to live full of lust and lies. Because misery loves company. If I don't live a pure life (my mind) and I don't care about honesty and integrity (my heart) then I won't be very motivated to right wrong—in mine or anyone else's life.

I continue to repeat that I am not talking about a perfect life with all sin obliterated, but I am saying, as does the Word, that we must be in the constant process of ridding ourselves of our own flesh and sin in order to be able to help anyone else. That's one of the practical reasons that there is a higher standard for leaders and teachers (James 3:1).

If you're an alcoholic and you decide you are ready to quit drinking, had you rather get help from a man that has been dry for three years and faithfully attends AA or a guy who can't remember where he spent last weekend? That's the point. None of us are sin-free, but when we are serious about living godly lives, we are more able and freed up to help others.

## DROP THE NETS

The Scriptures clearly tell us how we can slay the dragon of our own flesh on a daily basis.

*And so, dear brothers, I plead with you to give your bodies to God because of all he has done for you. Let them be a living and holy sacrifice—the kind he will find acceptable. This is truly the way to worship him. Don't copy the behavior and customs of this world, but let God transform you into a new person by changing the way you think. Then you will learn to know God's will for you, which is good and pleasing and perfect. Because of the privilege and authority God has given me, I give each of you this warning: Don't think you are better than you really are. Be honest in your evaluation of yourselves, measuring yourselves by the faith God has given us. —Romans 12:1–3 NLT*

So, how can you be a sacrifice and also be living at the same time? After all, a sacrifice is killed in a display of offering and worship. But all versions of this Scripture say a "living sacrifice." Paradox. Living while dying. Dying while living.

*Then he called the crowd to him along with his disciples and said: "If anyone would come after me, he must deny himself and take up his cross and follow me. For whoever wants to save his life will lose it, but whoever loses his life for me and for the gospel will save it. —Mark 8:34–35 NIV*

Here we go again! You take up a cross to go and die. That's what happened to Jesus. So, in effect, He is saying "follow me to your death, but in that, you will find life." A paradox. Living while dying. Dying while living.

If I want to save my life, I will lose it. But if I lose my life willingly, I will be saved. A paradox.

So in order to defeat our own flesh, we must decide to give up our life. There is a definite theme here that goes against everything our flesh tells us to do.

We've all heard what to do when we're driving on ice and lose control, right? We are told to lightly pump the brakes and steer *into* the skid. But what is the natural tendency when we are suddenly sliding off the road? Turn the steering wheel *away* and slam on the brakes! But to survive, we must do the opposite of what "feels" right and natural.

So, for a sacrifice to stay a sacrifice, yet still be living, then it must live on the altar. Stay on the altar 24/7. For you to be a living sacrifice, you must continually give up your desires for His destiny, handing over your lust for His life, and letting go of your own heart to take His hand.

*Walking along the beach of Lake Galilee, Jesus saw two brothers: Simon (later called Peter) and Andrew. They were fishing, throwing their nets into the lake. It was their regular work. Jesus said to them, "Come with me. I'll make a new kind of fisherman out of you. I'll show you how to catch men and women instead of perch and bass." They didn't ask questions, but simply dropped their nets and followed. A short distance down the beach they came upon another pair of brothers, James and John, Zebedee's sons. These two were sitting in a boat with their father, Zebedee, mending their fishnets. Jesus made the same offer to them, and they were just as quick to follow, abandoning boat and father. —Matthew 4:18–22* MSG

> FOR YOU TO BE A LIVING SACRIFICE, YOU MUST CONTINUALLY GIVE UP YOUR DESIRES FOR HIS DESTINY, HANDING OVER YOUR LUST FOR HIS LIFE, AND LETTING GO OF YOUR OWN HEART TO TAKE HIS HAND.

"Simply dropped their nets and followed" and "they were just as quick to follow, abandoning boat and father." Boat and father represents career and family. There's not much left after that, is there? This makes something so very difficult for these men sound so simple. Yet, this was their response to Jesus.

Let me ask you a question: What is it that you need to drop to really follow Christ? What's in your hands? What is holding you back? It doesn't even have to be a bad or evil thing. There was nothing wrong with being fishermen, nothing wrong with being in business with dad. That was a good, honest living. Jesus didn't spring them from jail to start a gang. He just called normal, simple men to start a revolution. That's what He's still doing today! He is calling you today to that same revolution. But are you holding on to anything that keeps you from joining up?

Not everyone that Jesus called dropped their nets.

*As they were walking along the road, a man said to him, "I will fol-low you wherever you go." Jesus replied, "Foxes have holes and birds of the air have nests, but the Son of Man has no place to lay his head." He said to another man, "Follow me." But the man replied, "Lord, first let me go and bury my father." Jesus said to him, "Let the dead bury their own dead, but you go and proclaim the kingdom of God." Still another said, "I will follow you, Lord; but first let me go back and say good-by to my family." Jesus replied, "No one who puts his hand to the plow and looks back is fit for service in the kingdom of God."—Luke 9:57–62 NIV*

At first read, these can make Jesus seem very harsh, but in every instance, the men were giving cultural excuses. He knew they were just trying to sound good and didn't mean what they were saying. Jesus had such a great way of saying, in essence, "Uh, cut the dung, guys. We both know what you're doing."

Now as for you, only you and God know what you need to do to become a living sacrifice. Only you and God know what you have to lose to find Him. What Goliath do you need to cut the head off of, so you can walk with Jesus in freedom? Before you can move on down the road of righting wrong, your heart has to be ready to go first.

Having made it this far in the book, you know we've talked plenty about giving up and letting go. We've also emphasized getting the help you need. But maybe in the *Live Pure* section, you fooled your-self into ignoring God's conviction, but now you can't. Maybe in the *Speak True* section, you lied to yourself and now you know the truth has to come out. Let Christ right your wrongs. It's what He does. It's why you need Him. Just crawl up on His altar and let Him take your life. As strange as that sounds, it will be the best decision you will ever make. Drop the nets before you get anymore tangled up in them.

If Jesus appeared to you right now and said, "Let's talk. Tell me what you need Me to do for you." What would you say? What would you hand over? What would need to be sacrificed? What would you want Him to change in you?

## Defeating the Me Monster

I titled this chapter, "Beware the Me Monster." Here's where I got that. My favorite mainstream comedian is Brian Regan. It's not real easy to make me laugh, and Brian can make me cry … laughing. When I watch Brian, I laugh at him and my family laughs at me for laughing. His bits on UPS, Little League, family vacations, and a myriad of other everyday topics make me laugh out loud even when I'm completely alone. He has one bit called "Dinner Party,"[8] (Youtube it.) and in it he talks about the Me Monster. That's the guy in the room that goes on and on talking about himself, what he's done, what he owns, where he's been, and how his life is so much better than anyone else's in the room. Well, there's a Me Monster in all of us. I'm a Me Monster. You're a Me Monster. It's a clever, funny way to describe our flesh. Because we like it when life's about us. We like it when we think others think life is about us. And we love a theology that tells us that God is all about what we want.

But to follow Jesus, the Me Monster that stands in defiance against the King of kings and taunts anyone to challenge him, well … he has to die. In fact, it is best if his head is cut off. There is only One Who can defeat the Me Monster. There is only One Who can right wrong. His name is Jesus. So crawl up on His altar. … I'll join you.

*Then I saw in the right hand of him who sat on the throne a scroll with writing on both sides and sealed with seven seals. And I saw a mighty angel proclaiming in a loud voice, "Who is worthy to break the seals and open the scroll?" But no one in heaven or on earth or under the earth could open the scroll or even look inside it. I wept and wept because no one was found who was worthy to open the scroll or look inside. Then one of the elders said to me, "Do not weep! See, the Lion of the tribe of Judah, the Root of David, has triumphed. He is able to open the scroll and its seven seals."*

*Then I saw a Lamb, looking as if it had been slain, standing in the center of the throne, encircled by the four living creatures and the elders.*

*… He came and took the scroll from the right hand of him who sat on the throne. And when he had taken it, the four living creatures and the twenty-four elders fell down before the Lamb. … And they sang a new song: "You are worthy to take the scroll and to open its seals, because you were slain, and with your blood you purchased men for God from every tribe and language and people and nation. You have made them to be a kingdom and priests to serve our God, and they will reign on the earth."*

*Then I looked and heard the voice of many angels, numbering thousands upon thousands, and ten thousand times ten thousand. They encircled the throne and the living creatures and the elders. In a loud voice they sang: "Worthy is the Lamb, who was slain, to receive power and wealth and wisdom and strength and honor and glory and praise!"*

*—Revelation 5:1–12 NIV*

## DISCUSSION QUESTIONS

1.  What is your favorite super-hero and why?

2.  Discuss the opening analogy on Page 153 regarding the identity of the Marines versus Christian brotherhood.

3.  What might a "bottom line brotherhood" for Christian men look like? What would our *"Semper Fi"* be?

4.  Answer the question on Page 156, "What would change in our world if we decided we were going to simplify and *Semper Fi* to agree that Jesus is Lord and that is the only hill we will all die on?"

5.  Why do you think we have allowed our differences as Christians to define us more than the unifying points?

6.  Discuss why we can often be pro-active in solving problems in so many scenarios, but have so much difficulty solving our own.

7.  Discuss this sentence from Page 163: "If I don't live a pure life (my mind) and I don't care about honesty and integrity (my heart) then I won't be very motivated to right wrong—in mine or anyone else's life." Agree? Disagree?

8.  Discuss Romans 12:1–3 and the concept of being a living sacrifice on Pages 163–164. Why is continually dying to ourselves so hard?

9.  Answer these questions from Page 165: "What is it that you need to drop to really follow Christ? What's in your hands? What is holding you back?"

10. Why is there no room in the Kingdom of God for the "Me Monster?" (p. 167)

    Close in prayer.

CHAPTER 13

# *RIGHT WRONG*
## SLAY THE DRAGONS

*"God love your soul and your aching bones.*
*Take a breath, take a step, meet me down below.*
*Everyone's the same, our fingers to our toes.*
*We just can't get it right, but we're on the road."* [1]
—*OneRepublic*

We've all seen the images and heard the stories of the knight slaying the dragon. We understand the dragon is a mythical creature, but it represents so many of our greatest fears. They're huge, they fly, they have claws, they're clever predators, and as if that wasn't bad enough, they breathe fire. So a giant lizard that can swoop down and swallow you, but can also set a city ablaze. Pretty scary stuff.

Since we dealt with our own hearts in the first *Right Wrong* chapter, next we're going to spend the second and final chapter of this tenet dealing with the other major relationships of our lives. There are dragons to slay today. No, they aren't scary giant lizards, they have different names now, but the fight is intense and we can still feel like we are being rained on by fire during the battle.

For the sake of time and space, I will only address common issues that I have personally seen plague us as men. There is a good possibility that I may not touch on a specific issue that you struggle with in one or more of your relationships. That is where I pray the Holy Spirit will speak to you here, even if your issue isn't mentioned. I also pray that there are principles you find here that will help you in those areas.

It is crucial to note, as we begin, that there is only so much you can do in making relationships right. But we are called to get things as right as we can. The end goal is our own hearts need to be made right with God and man. We are not responsible for the actions and choices of others, only our own. Check out this verse that has helped me a great deal in conflict resolution.

*If it is possible, as far as it depends on you, live at peace with everyone.* —*Romans 12:18* NIV

Notice Paul's quantifiers, "If it is possible" and "as far as it depends on you." In other words, do all you can, but let go of what you can't. There are times that physical distance or circumstances may prevent you from dealing directly with someone. And there are some people who are just not going to allow you to make it right.

If someone has died and you know your heart wasn't/isn't right, go to the gravesite, if it is physically possible. If not, speak out loud and talk to the person and God. Do what it takes for you to get right and be at peace!

I also believe this verse means to live at peace with yourself. So often, when we fail at reconciling with someone, then we beat ourselves up. If you have done all you can, then you must accept peace for yourself as well.

In our politically correct, don't-make-waves world, it is easy for us to believe that as Christians we should never have any enemies. That is a beautiful concept, but one very few people can pull off. Even Jesus didn't.

*But love your enemies, do good to them, and lend to them without expecting to get anything back.* —*Luke 6:35a* NIV

Notice Jesus didn't say, "don't have enemies." He assumed we probably would, so He told us what to do for them. A good definition of an enemy is someone who views you as a threat to him/her and treats you as such. Now, to be clear, this doesn't allow us to hate on people, but what to do when someone considers us as a threat to them.

## THE DRAGON TO SLAY FOR YOUR WIFE, YOUR BRIDE

If you are single and never been married, you still need to take in this section. Don't disregard it because you aren't married. It could help you immensely in starting and establishing your marriage someday. If you are single again, hopefully this information might help you on your path toward healing and rebuilding.

Now, let's talk about wives. The biggest issue for the man in his family is the art of leading. Yes, it is an art, because it is beautiful when someone knows what they're doing and really ugly when they don't.

Financial problems? Sexual issues? Career conflicts? Communication breakdown? These most often stem from leadership problems.

In the dysfunction department, there tends to be two overarching issues.

The first is the most common problem. The wife is leading and the husband isn't. Usually everyone knows it. The woman knows it. The kids know it. Other family members know it. People at church know it. The guy's buddies know it. But too often, the man is in denial.

Let's take a quick look at where this all started. And to set the record straight, Eve—and women—have gotten a lot of false blame over the centuries for the whole sin thing, but Eve wasn't the leader, was she? Where was Adam—the leader? Check out Genesis 3:6 NIV.

*When the woman saw that the fruit of the tree was good for food and pleasing to the eye, and also desirable for gaining wisdom, she took some and ate it. She also gave some to her husband, **who was with her,** and he ate it.*

Have you ever seen that before? Did you know Adam just sat there and watched the serpent play his wife? That he watched her take a bite, then offer him a bite? That scene wasn't as much about Eve's actions, but Adam's lack of action. Adam backed off and Eve stepped up. Places switched. Both stepped out of line. Chaos entered order. And therein, gentlemen, describes so many marriages in a nutshell, following the pattern set out for us in the Garden. How many marriages today reflect this scene of the man being passive, the woman leading, and the woman being blamed for the outcome. See it?

Why didn't Adam draw his sword and cut the head off the dragon … uh, serpent? Why didn't He call for God's help? When did he get lazy? Was it fear? Why didn't he right wrong—right then?! Bottom line is he didn't, so here we are.

**The first primary reason why a woman leads a family is laziness of the husband.**

I once asked a wife in a marriage counseling session this question: "Tell me the one thing you want to see your husband do?" She never hesitated as she answered, "I need him to man up!"

What causes us as men to not take the role God gave us at the marriage altar? Like with Adam, we ask "why?" Is it fear? Apathy? Self-image? What?

Although I haven't done a study of the Noland family tree and I can't judge family I never knew, I do know I am a first generation Christian in the sense of proclaiming to be a follower of Jesus, church-going, ministry-focused, tithing, etc. I do know I did not grow up in a Christian home, which you likely already sized up in previous chapters. My grandmothers on both sides went to church with some regularity, but my grandfathers didn't and no one on either side of the family ever spoke to me about Jesus, church, or anything on a spiritual level. Faith was never mentioned. Christianity was never on the family radar. I was on my own. So, at 19 years old, I decided to "drop my nets and leave boat and father," to follow Christ, which was not the norm for my family line.

Being a first generation Christian male is challenging and difficult. One of the biggest reasons is because you have no pattern to follow. But the advantage is … well, you have no pattern to follow. It forces you to look at Scripture and follow Jesus—no one else. You don't look around and wait for someone to join you, because there has been no one to join you before. You have no choice but to try and lead, because there is no one ahead of you to follow!

This path has been hard and I have made a lot of mistakes. … A lot of mistakes. I have quit, given up, taken a break, slacked off, and questioned why and how. But then I pick myself back up, allow God to dust me off, step back out in front of my family, ask for forgiveness, and move on. I would love to be able to say that I come from a long line of pastors and missionaries and sold-out warriors for Christ, but I don't. But I have also witnessed plenty of guys that do come from that family and seen it doesn't guarantee creating a family leader. It's a personal choice for each and every man.

Regardless of history, my responsibility now is to have that legacy begin with me. I have two boys. And, frankly, they don't care that I had no example. They want me to lead and they want me to show them how to lead. I have the opportunity through them to double the family legacy and then if each of them has two children … well, everything changes. If a hundred years from now, someone does a genealogy study of my family, they'll look at around 1979 and go, "Whoa! What happened here?!" Then in 1984 when I married a godly woman who shared my convictions, it secured a huge shift in the right direction.

So, what steps do you take to man up and lead when you haven't ever led or you haven't in a very long time?

First, communicate to your God. Repent of your laziness, disobedience, and for ignoring your duty as a Christian man. Good news though! There's not a single man in history that God hasn't forgiven when He has been asked. The other good news is that God can lead through you. You submit to Him, then He leads. So you lead by following and if you mess up, simply own up to it, and He forgives. Crawl back up onto the altar. You can complicate it if you choose to, but that's how it works—every time.

Second, communicate to your wife. Ask her to forgive you of the same things you asked God to forgive you for. But you should add the fact that you have not loved her to the level you need to. Leading your wife is loving your wife. Explain to her that you are concerned, afraid, and intimidated (if you are), but you really want to change and take your God-given role. Explain that she has done nothing wrong, but your lack of action has put a burden on her she shouldn't have had. You want to free her up to be the best wife, mother, and woman she can be. Most women are so grateful that God has answered their prayers that this will not be a bad meeting. If you're humble, she'll be helpful. If you're repentant, she'll resolve.

Third, communicate to your kids. You don't have to make a long speech. Just explain that they may notice some changes in how mom and dad do things. Tell them if they have any questions or don't understand something, to just ask. Explain that there may be some different spiritual aspects at home, but you need them to cut you some slack and be patient. Tell them that you are going to work hard to be more consistent and that they need to understand that is going to be best for everyone. Tell them that you are really wanting to be the best husband and dad you can be and that you want mom to be a happy woman and for them to be happy children. That's what this is all about.

**The second reason why a woman leads a family is the man's fear of the woman.**

This is a huge, rampant issue in our culture and one many men will deny. I've seen guys that are as big as linebackers living in constant fear of a 120-pound blonde. From my experience, most of us men battle with this issue on some level, but we hate to admit it. I have brought this topic up in men's groups and invariably there will be one guy who blurts out, "Well, I don't agree with that. I am not scared of my wife on any level." That is usually followed by multiple sets of eyes locking onto his and telepathically saying, "Dude, you are so afraid of her, it's not even funny!"

For men, the feeling of constantly failing often creates fear. Failing is either created by the fact that you actually have quite often or you just feel like you have. Regardless, chronic fear is unhealthy. If you are "walking on eggshells" with your wife, you cannot possibly be happily married. If when your wife says, "We need to talk," you feel like throwing up, that's a good sign you're standing on shaky ground.

Fear has to be replaced with respect and honor. As men, we understand respecting someone and honoring someone's position without being afraid of them. There is a big difference in a son who obeys dad because he is afraid of the consequences versus a son who obeys dad because he so deeply respects him. We understand that concept from bosses to teammates. When we fear our wives, we are not honoring them. We know that.

Getting with a few brothers and talking this issue through is really difficult, because it is so hard to admit, but it gets the problem outside of us. Then consistent prayer for grace, strength, and wisdom will help us grow. Being accountable for our words and actions with our wives can change the dynamics in our marriages faster than any other method for change.

Now, here's the other side of the coin.

There are men who rule with an iron fist and their wives are fearful, jumpy, and stressed out by their husbands. This is, of course, where in an extreme situation abuse can begin. But I am not talking about physical abuse here, simply a man lording over his wife and family with a "my way or the highway" approach. Guys, if this is you, you are out of balance in the other direction from fear. You are the source of fear. You have to begin to show respect and honor to your wife, allowing for her feelings and desires. You must learn to allow for her opinion and to value her thoughts, words, and actions. If a man says that doing these things is a sign of weakness, my response is that weakness is displayed when you can't honor anyone but yourself (Me Monster).

Honestly, all of us men lean toward one of these sides—fear or iron fist. Lean meaning a *tendency* toward one or the other.

After years of counseling and talking with couples of all ages, in my humble opinion, the number one thing a woman wants from her man is security. She is constantly saying in a thousand different ways, "Help me feel loved and safe." And yes, you may have accomplished that yesterday, but now she wants to know if you'll do it today too. It's not an event. It's a lifestyle. A woman whose husband is afraid of her and refusing to lead is making her feel unloved and insecure. A husband who is ruling with clenched teeth and a closed fist is making her feel unloved and insecure. An insecure woman will never be a fulfilled woman. A smile on her face doesn't always mean a smile in her heart.

My mentor often says, "You can see the character of a man in his wife's eyes." … Just let that one sit there for a minute. True and powerful.

*Submit to one another out of reverence for Christ. Wives, submit to your husbands as to the Lord. For the husband is the head of the wife as Christ is the head of the church, his body, of which he is the Savior. Now as the church submits to Christ, so also wives should submit to their husbands in everything. Husbands, love your wives, just as Christ loved the church and gave himself up for her to make her holy, cleansing her by the washing with water through the word, and to present her to himself as a radiant church, without stain or wrinkle or any other blemish, but holy and blameless. In this same way, husbands ought to love their wives as their own bodies. He who loves his wife loves himself. After all, no one ever hated his own body, but he feeds and cares for it, just as Christ does the church—for we are members of his body. "For this reason a man will leave his father and mother and be united to his wife, and the two will become one flesh." This is a profound mystery—but I am talking about Christ and the church. However, each one of you also must love his wife as he loves himself, and the wife must respect her husband. —Ephesians 5:21–33 NIV*

Years ago, as I began to be asked to officiate marriage ceremonies and my wife and I began to be asked to do pre-marital counseling, I searched desperately for a way to communicate this passage to couples and the delicate balance of mutual submission. Our culture has skewed this Biblical concept to seem archaic and it is often taken out of context from the way it was intended. So, in light of the confusion and controversy around this topic, I did a very strange thing—I just asked God to give me a picture I could share with couples that would make sense to them and override the cultural stigma. Here's what I heard very clearly: "ballroom dancing." After the proverbial "Whachu talkin' 'bout, Jesus?" I realized what He was saying.

Picture a large, darkened ballroom dance floor. The spotlight hits the middle of the wood and a couple strolls out to the center. He is in his tux and she in a beautiful, flowing gown. They look awesome. They know they look awesome. They clasp hands, embrace, and begin the dance. They move all around the floor with style and grace, giving the appearance of floating. They hover about effortlessly, both smiling and enjoying the experience. They are having fun. They are proud of what they have accomplished and what they are creating.

Now, at any point, does anyone watching them ask: "So, who's leading?" No. In ballroom dancing, everyone knows the man leads and the woman is following his moves. But when a couple is really good at this style of dancing, you can't tell who is leading. If both do what they are supposed to do while dancing, you are so mesmerized by the corporate effort of the two moving about as one that you aren't concerned or distracted by who is leading or following. It doesn't matter to anyone, because what is on display is beautiful. That's what the heart of Ephesians 5 is all about in regards to marriage.

Now, if the man decides he is tired of leading and stops, what happens? If she decides she is sick of following him, what happens? You got it. Not so pretty anymore. Suddenly those watching begin to concern themselves with the issue of whose at fault and what has gone wrong.

So, am I suggesting that you and your wife take ballroom dancing lessons? No, but I am asking you to consider this analogy to better understand Biblical submission and the role that you as your wife's husband should take. Do you need to get rid of some fear and sweep up some eggshells? Do you need to open your fist and hold your wife's hand? It's time to dance.

For followers of Jesus, He is both our example and goal. How would Jesus treat your wife differently than you do? What do you think He would recommend you change? And what would He affirm you in and tell you "good job" about?

I'll close the marriage section with something my wife and I tell every couple in pre-marital counseling after we read Ephesians 5 and share the ballroom dancing analogy. I look at the soon-to-be wife and say, "Your role to your husband will be to live for Him." Every time, the soon-to-be groom lights up. He looks at me like I just told him he could live in Hawaii for free. The goofy grin that washes over his face says, "Oh boy! That is so awesome! I love you so much for telling her that!" Then I look at him and say, "The Bible is clear on your role. While she is to live for you, you must die for her. Put her first always. Be willing to put your wants and wishes aside and do what is best for your bride. Just as Christ did and does for His Bride—the Church." Every time, his face falls. *"Die?"* The party is officially over. Ain't moving to Hawaii after all. But most every time, what comes next is a look of honor that sweeps over his countenance and he gets it—being a Christ-centered husband is a calling from God Himself!

> AS A CHRISTIAN MAN, LIFE IS NOT ABOUT US. WE PUT GOD FIRST, THEN OUR FAMILIES SECOND. THAT IS HOW WE LOVE HIM AND THEM. THAT IS HOW WE RIGHT WRONGS AND FOLLOW THE KING! THAT IS THE BEST WAY TO CHANGE THE WORLD!

Gentlemen, one thing is abundantly clear in Scripture—as a Christian man, it is not about us. We put God first, then our families second.

That is how we love Him and them. That is how we right wrongs and follow the King! That is the best way to change the world!

Next, after your bride, comes the kids …

## THE DRAGON TO SLAY FOR YOUR CHILDREN

The biggest thing we can do to right the wrongs in our children is to get ourselves right with God and healthy in spirit, and then get our marriage right and healthy, as we have previously covered. I am not going to launch into a comprehensive parenting session here. I am simply going to cover some basic principles for you as a father.

My wife and I have had this saying on our fridge for years: "Don't allow anything into your own life that you do not want reproduced in your children's lives." The idea being that those things we may be able to handle in moderation, our children may commit in excess. I'll let you apply your own examples from your life here, but it's a challenge to think this through and decide what is worth the risk to your children.

Let's go back to our lazy man/iron fist man examples from before. The majority of the time that a man rules his home with an iron fist, he is exasperating his children, while the man that is lazy and afraid of leadership is also lazy in his discipline and often afraid of his kids too.

The iron fist man cares about the rules, not the relationship, while the lazy man cares about the relationship and not the rules. Most lazy men want their kids to be their buddies to create less conflict, thus less work.

Author and communicator Josh McDowell has taught this family formula for years: "Rules without Relationship equals Rebellion."

I'll add the converse: Relationship with no Rules equals Running (all over you). The Biblical balance is Relationship with the Right Rules equals Righteousness.

James Dobson often shares this analogy, "Children are like the night watchman. They check all the doors, but they really don't want any of them to open." So often these actions are the child's heart asking, "Are you sure you love me and how much?" That simple truth has helped me greatly as a dad in interpreting my sons' motives and actions. Sometimes a child's behavior is rebellion that requires discipline and sometimes it is a request to be loved. The balance and wisdom lies in discerning the difference.

We know as children get older and make their own choices, they can stray from their foundation. Kids raised in godly homes get off course and can live life very different than mom and dad. And kids who grow up in horrible homes can turn out to be responsible, upright people. That is the exercise of free will. The possibilities are far better for the children to walk in health if mom and dad are and the younger you start, the better the opportunity. But as with anything in life, there are no guarantees.

Years ago, I was at a camp where a youth communicator had his three teenage sons with him for the week. As I observed them, I could tell they were godly, balanced young men. So I asked the dad a question I most always ask of good parents, "What's the best piece of parenting advice you can give me?" His answer: "Work your butt off when they're little and you're less likely to lose them when they're older."

I want to close this section with a practical exercise to help you and your kids constantly monitor where you are. Yes, I said where *you* are. Obviously, this exercise requires your children to be old enough and mature enough to converse on this level. If they are too young right now, plan on applying this down the road. But if you start young, they will get accustomed to this level of communication and it won't be so difficult later.

Sit your children down together. Tell them you are going to ask some questions and you want total honesty. Tell them they will not get in trouble for telling you the truth. You want the truth. (Gird your loins. It can hurt.) In this setting, there will be zero consequences for anything that is said. This is about getting the truth out and allowing you to know what wrongs you have done or are doing that must be made right. There may be some awkward silence, but plow through and stick with it. If you feel that one or more of your kids will do better one-on-one, then tell them you will be glad to speak with him/her alone after everyone is finished. But some shy children will speak up with the whole family where they won't alone. Regardless, it is important to have the corporate meeting first. There is power for them in numbers, regardless of the number. These meetings will get easier over time and hopefully make all communication better. It also gives your kids an outlet and a voice inside the family.

Ask them these questions:
—Tell me one thing that you believe I am doing right as a dad.
—Tell me one thing that you would like for me to stop or to change.
—Tell me one thing you need from me or want me to do for you.
—Tell me one way I can improve my relationship with you.

Feel free to ask your own questions. You get the idea. Realize that not too many dads sit down with their kids and ask for feedback, so right there you will be above the norm. Also, when they see you are serious about improving as a dad to this level, it communicates a great deal of care and validation to their feelings. Lastly, wouldn't you rather know exactly how they feel and deal with it, so you can be the best dad and the best example of Jesus you can be? As a Christian father, Job One is showing them the closest thing to their Heavenly Father that you can. (Chapter 4 should have driven the validity of that point home.)

## THE DRAGON TO SLAY FOR YOUR PARENTS

This can be the toughest place in our lives to right wrong, because the issues have been around for so long. Unhealthy family patterns may have been in place for decades with no change and no desire to change. There may have been an "elephant in the room" for a very long time, because no one wants to bring up the problems. This is where many men learn the dysfunction of denial. This is where many of our own wrongs began and then grew up with us. Even still, for us to really lead our own families in health, we must do all we can to make relationships right in the family we grew up in. Obedience can break down strongholds of the enemy that have existed for generations and stop them right here, right now.

In this section I will address the two major issues I have seen do the most damage to men and their own families. I realize these are very sensitive issues, but are also some of the most prevalent in our culture.

**First, men, you are no longer your dad or your mom's little boy.**

I'm not talking about hugging your dad or letting mom kiss you on the cheek. I'm talking about if they still treat you like a child when you are clearly a grown man. Don't play that game anymore and don't allow them to play it either. This issue can manifest itself in two ways—babying or bullying. Most often dad bullies and mom babies, but the opposite is certainly possible.

**Let's deal with Mom.**

Many times, I have seen a responsible grown man with a good job, nice home, a wife and three kids walk in where mom is and suddenly he's three-years-old again. She's doting and pampering and baby-talking. And he is allowing it and even playing into it some. Now, some men will say, "Well, why not? No one else treats me that way anymore." What is really interesting is that those same guys will often demand to be treated with a certain level of respect at their office, on their team, or in a church men's meeting, but not with mom.

There are few things a wife can loathe and disrespect more than her husband allowing mom to not recognize the man he is and allowing her to keep enabling the little boy syndrome. In fact, a lot of wives will at least understand a mother's heart and not blame the mom-in-law as much as her husband. But this can cause great damage to the relationship between a man's mother and his wife. If your wife has a problem with your mom and this is her reasoning, just know your wife is right, you are wrong, and mom needs to be gracefully put in her place. It's a hard talk, but it has to happen. If you married someone just like Mom and your wife has continued the babying, it's time to talk to your wife and your mom. Yes, it may be tough, but the proper respect and health are waiting on the other side of that talk.

**Now, let's deal with Dad.**

There are two possible dysfunctions here. As with mom, there are dads out there who will baby their sons. Actually it could be classified better as bailing out, rather than babying. That is mostly in the form of rescuing them out of bad situations and not allowing them out from under the parents' protection to experience the real world. In fact, a father bailing out his son can quickly enable poor behavior and choices. We raise our sons to become men, so enabling stunts the growth that God intends for them.

If dad keeps bailing you out, you must talk to him. Level with him. Speak the truth in love. It's time to let go and grow. Ninety-nine percent of dads will respect that you stood up and laid the issues on the table. He may even be relieved.

Or maybe you are the bailout dad. Talk to your son. It's time to let him grow up. Give the nod and turn Him over to Christ (Chapter 4).

Second, bullying from dad creates a boatload of issues in a male of any age. I have seen grown men live in fear of their father. He may have never even hit his son, but the verbal abuse and intimidation is devastating. Generally if this behavior begins as a boy, it often continues until the son puts a stop to it—even far into manhood. If you are being bullied by dad, sit down with him and communicate to say this has got to stop and why. Ending this dysfunction is going to help the entire family.

If you are the bullying dad, you need to get counseling to uncover where this started, deal with the root, and stop the behavior (Chapter 5).

Here's the bottom line to this over-all issue. If you feel like you are still just a child—at whatever age you are—to your father or your mother or both, then it is going to be difficult for you to lead your own family. If the two most important people in your development show you they don't believe you have grown up, that is a hindrance to your maturity.

Here's the really good news: God has ordained your marriage and made you and your wife one. If you have children, He has opened the womb of your wife and blessed you. God believes you can lead and He has ordained you to do so. What else do you need?

Go talk to mom and/or dad and get these or any other dysfunctional issues out in the open and straight. Yes, conflict and confrontation is always very hard, but everyone will feel better when the dysfunction ends. And your wife will totally respect you for taking charge of this lethal area. Also, you are less likely to repeat this behavior or allow it with your own children by ending the pattern with you.

## The Dragon to Slay for Your Circles of Influence

You know what a chameleon is, right? A fairly ugly lizard that changes colors depending on his surroundings. As guys, we can be social chameleons. Does your personality change according to your surroundings? Is the image you portray to friends—at work, in the neighborhood, at church, and in social circles—all the same guy? It is so tempting for us as men to show different sides of our personalities depending on what we believe the people in the room want to see. So we will change to please people.

Are you the funny guy in that room, but the spiritual guy in another room? Are you the quiet guy in this one, but the vulgar guy in that one? Are you the technical guy over here and the sports guy over there? Get the picture? No matter how much we may do this, deep in our heart, we don't like it. It just doesn't feel right. Why? Because God created each of us to be a whole and sole person, not eight versions of someone no one really knows. In trying to please everyone else, we are not being true to who we are.

I understand we have groups and places in our lives where certain topics are discussed. I'm also not talking about slight shifts in approach due to personality. We all have places we can "let our hair down" and places we are more reserved. I'm talking about major swings like an actor playing different roles.

So, here's a principle for you: Wherever you are, be the same guy. Don't give people who you think they want. Be who you are.

People like knowing what they're going to get when you're around. Don't make them guess who you're going to be. People will more likely respect you when they know what they're going to get, rather than causing them to constantly have to ask, "Who's he going to be this time?" And if someone doesn't like you? So what. Their loss.

If God wants someone else in a situation, He will put that person there. If He wants you there, then give them you. If He has ordained you to be in a certain place, then He needs you there. Be who He made you. If you are good enough for God, then why shouldn't you be good enough for you—and everyone else?

To support this point, look at the life of Jesus in the Gospels. He showed us so many different sides of His personality, yet He was always the definition of consistent. You just can't imagine the disciples asking, "Wow, I wonder what mood He's going to be in today?" No. Didn't happen. Or "Well, he's tried being funny with the Pharisees, then he tried acting smarter than them. That didn't work, so I wonder what He'll try next?" Nope. Never went down like that. They knew Who He was and the primary reason is He knew Who He was and He always presented exactly that! As you mature in Christ, you will find yourself becoming more balanced and more consistent. A definite sign of spiritual maturity is becoming confident in Him and comfortable in who you are.

*Jesus Christ is the same yesterday and today and forever.*
*—Hebrews 13:8 NIV*

## THE DRAGON TO SLAY FOR THE KINGDOM OF GOD

We are confined to this planet, in this world; however, as believers, we also live in God's Kingdom. We live in the world, but inside Christ—in His economy, in His protection, in His provision, in His mission, in His calling, in His life, and in His death.

How do we do this?

1.  **Apply His Word to your world**

*"Take to heart all the words I have solemnly declared to you this day, so that you may command your children to obey carefully all the words of this law. They are not just idle words for you—they are your life."*
                                            *—Deuteronomy 32:46–47a NIV*

*The Word of God is living and active. Sharper than any double-edged sword, it penetrates even to dividing soul and spirit, joints and marrow; it judges the thoughts and attitudes of the heart. —Hebrews 4:12 NIV*

I discovered a truth many years ago as I studied the Bible and was placed in the position of interpreting it into my life and others through ministry. It's this: God will never compromise His Word for anyone, but He will customize His Word for everyone. Allow me to explain.

> GOD WILL NEVER COMPROMISE HIS WORD FOR ANYONE, BUT HE WILL CUSTOMIZE HIS WORD FOR EVERYONE.

His laws, commands, precepts, and standards are true for us all. If the Word says it, then it applies to me, you, all of us. There is no compromising His Word. No changing the rules according to different situations or circumstances. No situational theology.

But if you and I read the same exact verses this morning, His Spirit can apply a custom message to both of us for our lives in that moment. We may get very different messages out of the same verses. The meaning is the same, the message can be different. Because His Word is interpreted to us by His Spirit, it can be used to speak in so many ways.

Here's an example. One man reads Psalm 37:4 NIV, *"Delight your-self in the Lord and he will give you the desires of your heart,"* and he hears God saying to him, "You've been trying to get your joy, your energy for life, from your job by working more and more and that is just not going to happen. Find your life in me." At the same time, another man opens his Bible and reads this verse and feels God say, "Believe that I want the best for you. Trust me that I will bring good things into your life." The Holy Spirit is customizing or targeting the needed message to each man's heart. What an awesome God!

There are thousands of principles and patterns in the Word for us to follow and live out. There is no compromise in these. Yet there are millions of potential customized messages from Him. This is why con-sistent reading and studying are so important. Yes, we should sit under strong Bible teaching, but we must learn the Scriptures for ourselves too.

**2.   Learn to hear His voice above any other voice**

Seeking wise counsel is vital to our life decisions. Communicating and discerning God's will with our wives is a crucial aspect of mar-riage. But, as leaders of our families and followers of Christ, we must listen to Him before anyone else. There are times everyone around us seems to know exactly what we should do. There are just as many times that no one seems to have any idea what we should do. In all situations, we must hear from God. We must know what He says.

*"The man who enters by the gate is the shepherd of his sheep. The watchman opens the gate for him, and the sheep listen to his voice. He calls his own sheep by name and leads them out. When he has brought out all his own, he goes on ahead of them, and his sheep follow him because they know his voice. But they will never follow a stranger; in fact, they will run away from him because they do not recognize a stranger's voice."*
—Jesus in John 10:2–5

What or who keeps walking up to your gate that you listen to? How many voices are clammering for your ear? How many people do you try and satisfy? Is there anyone or anything that keeps sneaking in the back door, so to speak, and grabs your attention? Whose voice is louder than Christ's in your life?

It is crucial to identify the voices around you that can get in the way of what God is saying to you. Some of them may need to be silenced, because they are wrong, while others need to be heard, but not necessarily heeded. In fact, the key isn't really to silence all other voices, but to so train yourself to always hear God above any other.

Let me give you an analogy. Let's say you are at a church picnic. Lots of people talking all around you and lots of children running and playing. Suddenly you hear a cry amidst the noise. You instantly know it is your child and something is wrong. You stop everything and start looking for him/her, right? That's the idea here. You can discern His voice over all others and you respond. You give God the availability to interrupt your life at any moment.

Here's another example. I am not nearly as busy as a lot of guys and my phone isn't constantly going off like a lot of men I know, but the most frequent and answered calls on my phone are my wife's. Why? Because of connection. Because of my need to hear her voice and her need to hear mine. It doesn't matter what the call is about, if at all possible, I answer. God should have that type of connection to us. When He calls, no matter what we're doing, we answer. Why? Because of connection. After all, isn't that what He does for us?

At the church I pastored, we would have an open mic testimony service a couple of times a year. On one particular Sunday, a woman who had become a Christian in the past two years got up to share. She told everyone that when she first came to church and I would say that God spoke to me, she would think I was crazy. She questioned that God truly spoke to me at all. I was just doing the "pastor thing." But she turned the corner and through tears said, "Since I've become a Christian, I don't think Robert is crazy anymore, because I know God speaks to people, because He speaks to me all the time now."

If we think that God is just a Sunday morning thing, then we are missing out on the greatest relationship of our lives.

### 3.   Accept who you are in Christ

*Everything that goes into a life of pleasing God has been miraculously given to us by getting to know, personally and intimately, the One who invited us to God. The best invitation we ever received! We were also given absolutely terrific promises to pass on to you—your tickets to participation in the life of God after you turned your back on a world corrupted by lust. So don't lose a minute in building on what you've been given, complementing your basic faith with good character, spiritual understanding, alert discipline, passionate patience, reverent wonder, warm friendliness, and generous love, each dimension fitting into and developing the others. With these qualities active and growing in your lives, no grass will grow under your feet, no day will pass without its reward as you mature in your experience of our Master Jesus. —2 Peter 1:3–8 MSG*

In the movie *Robin Hood: Prince of Thieves,* Kevin Costner states, "Nobility is not a birthright. It is defined by one's actions."[2]

God has given you the position and the authority as His son, but you also have the responsibility of living the life worthy of that calling. I understand that it is a tough and taxing role to walk this faith life out daily. We can feel very alone and isolated. We can look around at our jobs, among our friends, even in our churches, and ask, "Okay, so who else is really doing this? Does anybody else really care about faith?" Let's look at another simple analogy.

Regardless of where we live, we have all been in plenty of stores and restaurants where we have encountered the employee that displays the attitude of "I could care less that I'm at work and that you are my customer right now." We have all dealt with that scenario far more times than we want to recall.

However, have you encountered the opposite? You go into a store or pull up to the drive-thru window and here is a beaming, bright person that makes you think they got out of bed this morning just to have the pleasure and the privilege of serving you. He/she makes you believe that they want nothing more than to take care of whatever you want while you are in their presence. When we get to be around an employee like this, we are amazed. Why? Because it just doesn't happen very often in this culture anymore. So really, sticking out like that isn't that hard, is it? You just have to be a gentle, polite, caring person who sincerely loves people and wants to help. Does that/shouldn't that describe us as Christians anywhere we are?

St. Francis of Assisi once said, "Preach the Gospel everywhere and if necessary, use words." That's not meant to be used as a free pass for us to not share our faith, but rather a check to make sure our words back up our actions.

In the suburb in which I live, we had a national chain office supply store open up. After several trips there, I realized I had yet to see a crabby employee. Everyone was friendly and seemed like they cared. One morning I asked for the manager and you could tell, sadly enough, that everyone thought a complaint was coming. He approached me and asked how he could help. I said, "Just have a quick question. Since you have opened here, everyone has a great customer service mindset and I want to ask you how you achieved this across the board with your employees?" He didn't hesitate in answering, "When I do interviews, I'm not really looking for experience or ability, I'm looking and listening for attitude. If I pick up on a positive, healthy attitude, I hire them. Because I can train someone like that to do anything. But if they have a poor attitude in the interview, I don't care how much experience or skill they have because I've learned I can't change that in an employee."

*"So, Robert, what does this talk about employees and attitudes have to do with me accepting who I am in Christ?" … Everything.*

*Your attitude should be the same as that of Christ Jesus: Who, being in very nature God, did not consider equality with God something to be grasped, but made himself nothing, taking the very nature of a servant, being made in human likeness. —Philippians 2:5–7 NIV*

*Therefore, since Christ suffered in his body, arm yourselves also with the same attitude, because he who has suffered in his body is done with sin. —1 Peter 4:1 NIV*

*You were taught, with regard to your former way of life, to put off your old self, which is being corrupted by its deceitful desires; to be made new in the attitude of your minds; and to put on the new self. —Ephesians 4:22–24a NIV*

Did you think I might go into a deep, theological dissertation of explaining who you are in Christ? There are many great books out there on that very topic. I chose a much simpler approach, and honestly, who can't make an attitude adjustment? And how much of our faith is reflected to the world from our attitude?

So here's a closing question for you. How many wrongs could be made right in your marriage, your children, your job, your friends, your church, and your circles of influence just by an attitude adjustment? Not a giant to-do list of changes, just simply attitude.

Gentlemen, our job on this earth is to be a force of righteousness to change things into the way God would have them. That is exactly our identity and who we are in Him! It starts with us, then our families, then our circles of influence, and into the world.

There are wrongs today in our own lives, in our families, in our circles, in the world that God fully intends for you and me to make right. The only question is, will we?

## DISCUSSION QUESTIONS

1.   Discuss Romans 12:18 on Page 171: *"If it is possible, as far as it depends on you, live at peace with everyone."* and Luke 6:35a: *"But love your enemies, do good to them, and lend to them without expecting to get anything back."* Talk about the concept of "enemies" in today's world.

2.   Why do you think spiritual leadership of the family is such a difficult struggle for so many of us?

3.   Discuss these questions from Page 173: "What causes us as men to not take the role God gave us at the marriage altar? Like with Adam, we ask 'why?' Is it fear? Apathy? Self-image? What?"

4.   Discuss the concept from Pages 175–176 regarding men being fearful of their wives. How does failure factor into this issue?

5.   Do you tend to be a "walk on eggshells" husband or an "iron fist" husband? Explain.

6.   Discuss the "ballroom dancing" analogy from Page 178. Agree? Disagree? Why?

7.   Answer these questions from Page 179: "How would Jesus treat your wife differently than you do? What do you think He would recommend you change?"

8.   What is your biggest struggle in being a dad? If you could change one thing right now in your fatherhood, what would it be?

9.   Talk about your biggest struggle as an adult that you have with your parents.

10.  Discuss what you can do as Christian brothers to help your attitudes be "the same as Christ Jesus."

Close in prayer.

CHAPTER 14

# *Follow the King*
## As For Me and My House

*"I'll help you break the walls down.*
*And bust you out and take you home.*
*Believe you me, you're not alone.*
*I'll help you break the walls down."* [1]
—*The Rocket Summer*


Have you ever thought about the difference between Peter and Judas? They began to follow Christ around the same time. They appeared to start off their journey with Jesus on the same level, both being given responsibility in His ministry. But near the end of Jesus' time on this planet, just before the crucifixion, their lives took very dramatic turns. In the Garden, Judas sealed his betrayal of Christ, while Peter jumped between Jesus and the soldiers, swinging a sword. In the courtyard, Peter briefly joined Judas' betrayal by his denials, yet who was nearest to Jesus—at least physically—at the beginning of the trials? Peter. Yes, he denied Christ to save his own hind-end, but give him some credit for being the closest one to the fray. Then, not long after this, Peter began his journey to become the Rock of the Church, while Judas took his own life in shame, guilt, and regret.

But these guys started out on equal footing just a few years before, didn't they? So what happened? What causes one man to take such a very different road than another?

Today, what causes two guys to accept Christ at the same time and one becomes a leader, while the other stays status quo? Two men join a Bible study group and one eventually drops out and disappears, while another can't seem to get enough of God. Of course, depending on your theological leanings, you factor in God's sovereignty on some level in this question. But if you believe that God gives us free will to make choices about Him and that Jesus came to offer all men the same opportunity to know Him, then the bottom line is that some men take Him up on His offer and some don't. It may take a while to see the truth in someone's life, but eventually one way or the other wins out. Some men choose to follow the King and some don't. Scripture tells us in a number of places that some will appear to be followers, but it will be seen in the end that they truly are not. The outward may appear very spiritual, but in reality is not at all. It is a façade.

*By their fruit you will recognize them. Do people pick grapes from thornbushes, or figs from thistles? Likewise every good tree bears good fruit, but a bad tree bears bad fruit. A good tree cannot bear bad fruit, and a bad tree cannot bear good fruit. Every tree that does not bear good fruit is cut down and thrown into the fire. Thus, by their fruit you will recognize them. "Not everyone who says to me, 'Lord, Lord,' will enter the kingdom of heaven, but only he who does the will of my Father who is in heaven. Many will say to me on that day, 'Lord, Lord, did we not prophesy in your name, and in your name drive out demons and perform many miracles?' Then I will tell them plainly, 'I never knew you. Away from me, you evildoers!'* —Matthew 7:16–23 NIV

Passages like this are some of the scariest in Scripture. At least they are to me. How many guys do you know that prophesy, drive out demons, and perform miracles? That's some serious evidence, yet Jesus says that doesn't get you the key to His Kingdom. But if that guy came to your church, how long would it take before he was placed into leadership?

Now look at where Jesus goes from here …

## HE THAT HAS EARS TO …

*"Therefore everyone who hears these words of mine and puts them into practice is like a wise man who built his house on the rock. The rain came down, the streams rose, and the winds blew and beat against that house; yet it did not fall, because it had its foundation on the rock. But everyone who hears these words of mine and does not put them into practice is like a foolish man who built his house on sand. The rain came down, the streams rose, and the winds blew and beat against that house, and it fell with a great crash." —Matthew 7:24–27 NIV*

What does Jesus say makes the difference in the man whose house survives the flood and the one that doesn't? The one who enters the Kingdom of Heaven and the one that doesn't? Look at the first sentence. The man who is known as wise, whose house survives, and gets into the Kingdom of God does two things:

1.   He hears Jesus' words.

2.   He puts Jesus' words into practice.

May I be so bold here—while subjecting myself to the potential criticisms of those who are sensitive to the grace/works issue—and say it comes down to personal obedience. Personal choice. … Okay, let's cover the bases … Am I saying it is all about us? NO! This is still all about God. Without Him speaking, there is nothing. It started that way in Genesis 1 and it is still that way. Am I saying we earn a place with Him by our works? NO! We already have that place by His grace and gift of salvation—if we have indeed chosen it. I'm talking about responding to our Lord out of gratitude and calling. Am I saying that we have a choice of who to listen to, who to obey, and whose foundation on which we build our personal house? YES! We place our faith in God's words, not in our ability to build our own house. Our house falls down in the flood. A Jesus house stands.

Let's take Point 1 apart—Jesus speaks.

Just like in any relationship, we have the choice as to whether we listen, but then also *hear*. Especially as guys, we listen all the time, but that is no guarantee that we hear. We can be aware that someone is speaking to us, but then when they ask us what was just said, we can show that we have no clue. When the TV or the radio is on, are we always hearing what is said? Of course not. Listening, probably. Hearing, no. So when Jesus speaks to us, we must listen and hear. Take it in. Consider what He says. Like He often said, "He that has ears to hear, let him *hear.*"

Now, Point 2—Put His words into practice.

Practice like a doctor or a lawyer, not a sports team. We're not getting ready for the big game, we are in the big game. Putting His words into action in our lives. Remember in Chapter 1 when we talked about ignorance to knowledge to application? This is exactly what Christ is communicating here. He tells us something we did not know or did not yet know to do (ignorance to knowledge), then we put those words into practice (knowledge to application). We apply His words. We obey His instruction. We take action in His name.

How does a coach know during the game which players *heard* him in practice? How does an employer know during business hours which employees *heard* him in the store meeting? How does a pastor know on Saturday who *heard* his plea for help about the service day that he announced last Sunday? How does a wife know her husband *heard* her when she asked him to take out the trash? It's funny how when we apply this simple logic to our relationship with Jesus, we want to get all theological and debate viewpoints, don't we?

Try that with your wife the next time she asks you to take out the trash. *"Well, honey, I can't actually respond to your request until we discuss the dynamics of the trash bag and deal with the question of when is it really full? At what point do you consider it filled versus when I think it is filled? Do we put the trash out on the curb tonight in faith that the trash man will come tomorrow or do we take it out in the morning out of works when we see the truck coming? Do we take it to the curb on our own or should we live in the hopes he will come to the garage and get it?"* … Ridiculous? Yeah, very. Would you do this? No, of course not. But how much of all our debating sounds like trash talk to God, when meanwhile He is speaking and His words aren't being heard? … and applied? On that note …

Remember the guys that had prophesied, cast out demons, and performed miracles that Jesus said He didn't know? It certainly sounded like they had heard and obeyed, didn't it? Evidently they managed to either do this under some other power or they did it in their own name, for their own glory. But as with most situations, Jesus is talking about a lifestyle, a practice of doing things outside of Him and outside of a relationship with Him.

Let's look farther into Matthew at Chapter 25.

*"When the Son of Man comes in his glory, and all the angels with him, he will sit on his throne in heavenly glory. All the nations will be gathered before him, and he will separate the people one from another as a shepherd separates the sheep from the goats. He will put the sheep on his right and the goats on his left. "Then the King will say to those on his right, 'Come, you who are blessed by my Father; take your inheritance, the kingdom prepared for you since the creation of the world. For I was hungry and you gave me something to eat, I was thirsty and you gave me something to drink, I was a stranger and you invited me in, I needed clothes and you clothed me, I was sick and you looked after me, I was in prison and you came to visit me.' "Then the righteous will answer him, 'Lord, when did we see you hungry and feed you, or thirsty and give you something to drink? When did we see you a stranger and invite you in, or needing clothes and clothe you? When did we see you sick or in prison and go to visit you?' "The King will reply, 'I tell you the truth, whatever you did for one of the least of these brothers of mine, you did for me.' "Then he will say to those on his left, 'Depart from me, you who are cursed, into the eternal fire prepared for the devil and his angels. For I was hungry and you gave me nothing to eat, I was thirsty and you gave me nothing to*

*drink, I was a stranger and you did not invite me in, I needed clothes and you did not clothe me, I was sick and in prison and you did not look after me.' "They also will answer, 'Lord, when did we see you hungry or thirsty or a stranger or needing clothes or sick or in prison, and did not help you?' "He will reply, 'I tell you the truth, whatever you did not do for one of the least of these, you did not do for me.' "Then they will go away to eternal punishment, but the righteous to eternal life." —Matthew 25:31–46 NIV*

Maybe I am just too simplistic in my personal study and theology, but doesn't the difference in the two groups come down to one group doing the things Jesus would do, while the other didn't? … Now, before you call the theology police about a Code E2:8–9—works/grace violation, hear me out. Actually, the reality of the two groups is one is filled with and motivated by the Spirit of God to bring His Kingdom to Earth (as it is in heaven), while the other is not filled with His Spirit, therefore there is no reflection of the work His Spirit accomplishes. That, my friend, is not about works, but about lining up with and obeying His Spirit that is alive within you … or not.

Could this be the difference in the demon casting guys and the disciples (who also cast out demons)? Yes. Could this be the difference in the guys with the house on the rock and sand? Yes. Could this be the difference in the sheep and goats? Yes. And the difference in Peter and Judas? Yes. Gentlemen, it appears that our obedience to God is crucial to what He can accomplish through us. The willingness of the vessel determines the flow.

If you've made it this far in the book, you have waded through a lot of issues and questions. But it would be a tragedy and a travesty if you seriously dealt with purity issues, truth issues, and righting wrongs throughout your life, but missed Jesus. Evidently by the passages we have just read, it can be done and is done by many. I believe that is why Jesus called His way the narrow road that few would find (Matthew 7:13–14).

One thing is for sure—regardless of who you are, your background or belief, we are all serving and worshipping something. It's just a matter of what it is and whether it matters in the end or not.

> REGARDLESS OF WHO YOU ARE, YOUR BACKGROUND OR BELIEF, WE ARE ALL SERVING AND WORSHIPPING SOMETHING. IT'S JUST A MATTER OF WHAT IT IS AND WHETHER IT MATTERS IN THE END OR NOT.

I want to pause here and repeat my plea from Chapter 1 and this will be the last time in the book. If you do not have a personal relationship with Jesus Christ, can you think of a better time than right now to begin? Page 233 has some basic information on how to become a Christ follower. There is also a prayer to help you if you are ready to start down His road for the first time or maybe you've walked away at some point and you need to return to Him. Pray and get honest with Jesus. Then tell someone you know who follows Him about your decision as quickly as possible. In fact, calling someone after you pray is a great thing. To immediately declare what you have decided. "I just called to say I have decided to follow Jesus" is a great message for a believer to receive.

Pray, receive, tell. ... moving on now.

## IT'S YOUR CALL

In medieval days, a knight was sworn to the allegiance of the King of his nation. He was sworn to uphold his laws and commands, to defend the King and country with his very life. He had no choice in this because of his station, even if the king was evil. Therein lies some of the greatest news of the Gospel. Jesus Christ, the King of kings and Lord of lords, is the perfect King. Right, just, fair, loving, graceful, merciful. He is Father, Healer, Comforter, and Creator. What king in the history of the world can make those claims? What followers can make that claim of their king? None. That is why ...

*Therefore God exalted him to the highest place and gave him the name that is above every name, that at the name of Jesus every knee should bow, in heaven and on earth and under the earth, and every tongue confess that Jesus Christ is Lord, to the glory of God the Father.* —Philippians 2:9–11 NIV

As a man with a free will and the choice as to how to live your life, why should you crawl up on His altar, sacrifice your own life and ego, and spend the rest of your days walking with Him in obedience, hearing and applying His words? Please allow the rest of this book to both challenge and inspire you to join Joshua as he said …

*"As for me and my household, we will serve the Lord."* —Joshua 24:15 NIV

*"As for me and my family, we'll worship God."* —Joshua 24:15 MSG

## The King is worthy to follow because He changes … Pagans into Priests

I have a lot of friends who are in full-time ministry—from pastors to para-church, from managers to missionaries. Some are rookies with just a few years in service, while others are like myself with 30+ years and counting. One of the commonalities I know about them all is that, regardless of their back story, each one would tell you, as I would, that their hearts have been, at many points in life, very far away from the God we serve. There are many days that we feel more like pagans than priests. But it's not about feelings. And not even about the job we do, but about our hearts.

I share this observation to make a simple point—Scripture is clear that regardless of vocational calling, *any* man that accepts Christ as Lord turns from pagan to priest. What you do for a paycheck, whether clerk, corporate, construction, or clergy doesn't matter as much as the purpose of your life being to serve Him and bring His will to Earth. What you do for a living just finances that ministry.

*But you are a chosen people, a royal priesthood, a holy nation, a people belonging to God, that you may declare the praises of him who called you out of darkness into his wonderful light. Once you were not a people, but now you are the people of God; once you had not received mercy, but now you have received mercy. Dear friends, I urge you, as aliens and strangers in the world, to abstain from sinful desires, which war against your soul. Live such good lives among the pagans that, though they accuse you of doing wrong, they may see your good deeds and glorify God on the day he visits us. —1 Peter 2:9–12 NIV*

Jesus turns us from men who do not—or will not—acknowledge God into men called and ordained into His service. No matter who told you that you were a winner or worthless, whether you were first string or third string, A-List or D-List, no longer matters. In Christ, you count. You matter. He assigns you as a priest into His Kingdom. A priest has the authority and ability, not only to speak to Him directly anytime, but also to intervene on His behalf in people's lives. Christ's work on the cross tore the curtain between God and man, so any man who receives Christ can go straight to Jesus for himself, his family, and for anyone God calls that man to minister to (Matthew 27:50–51, Hebrews 4:15–16).

What does a pagan do? Whatever he wants, because life is meaningless and there is no God. Does anything truly matter when there is nothing past this life? No.

What does a priest do? He does the will and the work of God. What really matters when eternity is at stake? Everything.

Therefore, God wants to use you to right wrongs, to be His agent of change in the world and His Kingdom. He wants you to hear Him, apply His words, which will bring His Kingdom to Earth. Redeem the lost. Save the perishing. Rescue the captives. By Him and in His name. What a noble calling! Gentlemen, this is the only sure way I know of to be certain you don't waste your life! You get to the end of the race and you don't look back in regret. You hit the tape ready to face Him. Why? Because you followed the King to the end.

*I have written you quite boldly on some points, as if to remind you of them again, because of the grace God gave me to be a minister of Christ Jesus to the Gentiles with the priestly duty of proclaiming the gospel of God, so that the Gentiles might become an offering acceptable to God, sanctified by the Holy Spirit. Therefore I glory in Christ Jesus in my service to God.* —Romans 15:15–17 NIV

Men, our glory is not on a battlefield like the knights of old, but it is found in the life of our King, Who has called us to His service, as Paul stated so well.

## THE KING IS WORTHY TO FOLLOW BECAUSE HE CHANGES ... PRODIGALS INTO PRINCES

I have shared some of my story throughout this book and here I want to tell you about the major spiritual turning point for me. I suppose it is arguable if I am a true prodigal in the Biblical view of the word or if I just didn't fully understand the Christ-life at age 12. But by the sixth grade, I had never darkened the door of a church. Some friends invited me to what they called, "Sunday school." ... (Can I just say as a lost kid that does not sound appealing on any level?) But as with most of us, relationships win out and I went anyway. The dozen or so young boys all herded into this little room and the "teacher" began to speak. He talked about things that we do wrong. I quickly noted that I had done some bad things. (Okay, he had me.) Then he said that those things made the God Who created us very unhappy. ... (Dang! I just found out there's a God and now He's already upset with me. I didn't even know He existed a few minutes ago. Not good.) But wait, then he told us that this God came down in the form of a man named Jesus and He sacrificed His life for mine, so I wouldn't have to go to Hell. (I had heard of that place before, but now it made sense that people tell you to go there when they're ticked at you.)

Now let's review: I do bad things that God doesn't like and that condemns me to a place of eternal fire, because He is perfect and just. But He made a way to fix this situation through believing that His Son died in my place, so I wouldn't have to, because He is loving and merciful. He makes a place for me in His home in Heaven. … Hmmm. … Sounds like a no-brainer. Wonder what the catch is? Oh well, count me in.

That was quite literally my 12-year-old brain's thought process. Now, here's the dilemma. I prayed the prayer, but never understood this offer included a life that could be lived with this God. I heard one-time event, when it was really a lifelong relationship.

Fast forward to barely 19-years-old. Now I'm a musician who just wants to be a rock star. (Think early '80s glam-rock bands.) I am far away from God, the church, the Bible, all things Christian. (Yes, that includes actual Christians.) I get invited to go play drums on a church choir trip by a minister that had the guts to reach out past the protocols and norms of the traditional church. Much to my surprise and threat to my personal hip factor, I accepted. That week, I hung out with Christians, played at a church every night, and was re-introduced to Scripture. I got loved on in spite of myself. I was cared for just for who I was, not what I did. Man, who does that?! About four nights in, a "light bulb" went off in my spirit. The reason that the last seven years had been miserable is because I was on the wrong road. You know how when you realize you're lost on a highway and can't figure out if you should just keep driving or turn around, but you know you have no clue where you are? That was me doing life. Well, I came home and did a 180-degree turn. Walked away from my past life and walked into a new life. I hated that I had wasted several years, but I was thankful I was finally shown the right road. I was thankful the same Father that made sure I heard about Him, also made sure I was able to make my way back to Him, to find my way home.

Here's another young man who found his way home too.

*Jesus continued: "There was a man who had two sons. The younger one said to his father, 'Father, give me my share of the estate.' So he divided his property between them. "Not long after that, the younger son got together all he had, set off for a distant country and there squandered his wealth in wild living. After he had spent everything, there was a severe famine in that whole country, and he began to be in need. So he went and hired himself out to a citizen of that country, who sent him to his fields to feed pigs. He longed to fill his stomach with the pods that the pigs were eating, but no one gave him anything. "When he came to his senses, he said, 'How many of my father's hired men have food to spare, and here I am starving to death! I will set out and go back to my father and say to him: Father, I have sinned against heaven and against you. I am no longer worthy to be called your son; make me like one of your hired men.' So he got up and went to his father. "But while he was still a long way off, his father saw him and was filled with compassion for him; he ran to his son, threw his arms around him and kissed him. "The son said to him, 'Father, I have sinned against heaven and against you. I am no longer worthy to be called your son. "But the father said to his servants, 'Quick! Bring the best robe and put it on him. Put a ring on his finger and sandals on his feet. Bring the fattened calf and kill it. Let's have a feast and celebrate. For this son of mine was dead and is alive again; he was lost and is found.' So they began to celebrate. —Luke 15:11–24 NIV*

The story of the Prodigal Son is one of the most well-known in the Bible. The term "prodigal" has come to mean a grown child who had followed the faith of his/her parents, then walked away to choose another lifestyle. The term itself doesn't assume the "coming home" part. If someone today says, 'I have a prodigal son or daughter," they mean their child has strayed from the belief in which they were raised. That is most often followed by a parent's sentiment of "watching the road" for that child to come back home—to family and faith. But the sad reality is someone can die a prodigal.

Some of you reading this book have a Prodigal Son testimony, whether that be from many years of rebellion or a brief trek on the wild side in college. Some of you may be a Prodigal who hasn't found his way home yet. I pray you find your way back home to who you truly are.

Aside from this most understood connotation, I want us to consider that all men are prodigals in two ways.

First, God created each of us to have fellowship with Him. When He formed us in our mothers' wombs, He had high hopes for us to spend our lives with Him. But the sin nature drove us to "leave home" and explore the world. Some come home when they're six years old, some as teens, while others as grown men. Sadly, some never make it back home. But, regardless, that length of time from creation to new creation is a prodigal season for God as Creator and Father. Waiting and watching, but always working on our behalf, until we come home—or it's too late.

For the second point, I'll make it a personal example. On any given day, I awake as a born-again Christ follower, but within a few hours … okay, sometimes only minutes … I make a choice to "leave home" and take my own path. My motive, attitude, and action causes me to turn my back on my Father, my God, and takes me to a foreign land, away from His presence, by my own choice. Whether that is minutes, hours, or days living in that choice and state of sin, I can then be convicted, repent, and return home. He receives me with open arms. … See it? The prodigal process is constantly occurring in our hearts, even when sometimes, the only ones that know it is us and the Father. Throughout our lives, God constantly desires that this Prodigal time become shorter and shorter. The cross allows for us to come back home, anytime, even many times a day.

Whether you agree with this notion doesn't really matter, because here's the real point. The focus of this passage is not so much about the son's disobedience, but the father's response. Jesus didn't tell this story to prove how detrimental sin is. He told the story to display the depth of His Father's love. The depth of His love. That's the point.

No matter how long we're gone, how far we fall, how deep we dive, or how depraved the disobedience, He is there. He has already made provision for the redemption of our souls. He has already taken back the keys to death and Hell. He has paid for every debt that we could possibly owe in our bankrupt hearts.

> NO MATTER HOW LONG WE'RE GONE, HOW FAR WE FALL, HOW DEEP WE DIVE, OR HOW DEPRAVED THE DISOBEDIENCE, HE IS THERE.

So what does God do when we come home? As in Jesus' parable, He restores us not to servanthood, but to full sonship. He wraps us with His robe of righteousness. He puts the ring with His seal on our finger, allowing us to be involved in His work, accomplishing His purposes by His Name (2 Corinthians 5:21, Ephesians 4:24).

If one of my sons leaves home and goes the wrong way, is he still my son, bearing my name? Yes, of course. His decision may create consequences, but it doesn't change who he is.

It is not about what we believe we deserve or don't deserve, it is about what God wants for our lives. It is not about what we have done or not done, but about what God has accomplished for us. He offers each of us as men—every moment of every day—the opportunity to no longer be prodigals in search of significance and satisfaction, but to be princes—sons of the King—acting under His authority.

But, first, we have to head down the road towards Home, towards the Father. Repent. About face. Turn around.

*"Hey there! All who are thirsty, come to the water! Are you penniless? Come anyway—buy and eat! Come, buy your drinks, buy wine and milk. Buy without money—everything's free! Why do you spend your money on junk food, your hard-earned cash on cotton candy? Listen to me, listen well: Eat only the best, fill yourself with only the finest. Pay attention, come close now, listen carefully to my life-giving, life-nourishing words. I'm making a lasting covenant commitment with you, the same that I made with David: sure, solid, enduring love. I set him up as a witness to*

*the nations, made him a prince and leader of the nations, And now I'm doing it to you.* —Isaiah 55:1–4 MSG

## The King is worthy to follow because He changes ... Lepers to Leaders

I don't know about you, but I have never had a terminal skin disease where you lose feeling in your extremities and then ultimately lose limbs. I have never felt the shame and rejection from people who wouldn't come near me, touch me, or even look at me.

Leprosy was a very common, but very serious health threat in the days of Jesus. It created a society of people who were shunned by the masses, left to devastating isolation and loneliness, desperately in need of love and healing. For that very reason, Jesus spent a good amount of time with them (Luke 7:21–22).

Bottom line is no one *chose* to be around a leper ... except Jesus. When everyone was running from them, He was walking towards them.

Changing gears now—leaders are people who go before others to blaze trails, make new paths, and discover uncharted territory. If we call someone a leader, we are also saying that someone is following.

I have a friend that says, "If you think you're a leader, but you look behind you and no one is following, then guess what? You're not a leader. But if you don't believe you're a leader, yet you look behind you and people are following, then guess what? You're a leader!" So, ultimately, it's not so much about the perception of the person leading, as it is about the followers.

That's what makes Twitter so interesting. Sure there are people who use it for just another way to stay in touch with friends on the little things of life. (If it's big, then you would at least text, right?) But celebrities can collect huge amounts of followers. Why? Because we like to think that if our favorite actor, rock star, or sports celebrity just saw something, thought something, ate something, or experienced something, we could be the first people on the planet—along with his/her other 685,000 followers—to hear about it! That makes us feel so special! We are in their (very large) inner circle. But that is leading. Why? People are following.

Christ can take men like me and you and turn us from shunned, rejected, and unloved spiritual, social, and emotional lepers into leaders. Men others want to follow.

I can write down a list of men's names that just a few years ago, if you had looked at their lives, I couldn't have paid you to follow them. Enter Jesus. These men each responded with obedience to Him. He began to heal them. They began to grow and mature. Now their families and a growing circle of people from employees to friends to other followers of Christ will listen to them, respect them, and yes, even follow them. What made the difference between modern-day "leper" and leader for these men? Christ. Period.

When I was pastoring, there was a family that had joined the Body. The man/husband/dad was a very happy-go-lucky guy that was well-liked, but he kept everyone at arms length. Well, life wasn't going very well and finally, he allowed me into the truth. They were going to lose their home, their cars, and they had no money in the bank. They both had jobs, but life was going down fast. To spare the gory details, this guy decided it was time to change. ... Oh no! The "C" word!

He began to talk to and listen to his God. He began to read and apply Scripture. He began to submit his life to other men. He began to enter into accountable relationships for the purpose of protection and growth. He began to heed the wisdom of a multitude of counselors. He began to pay attention to his family. People started to matter. His heart began to change. The "leper" was getting his feeling back. Healing was coming. Slowly, his family began to pull together. God was at work.

Through his new and growing relationship with God, this man was led to begin a business that serves the mentally and physically challenged in our culture by finding them jobs. Today, that company is adding employees by the week and expanding into other cities. And the coolest thing of all is if you ask him right now, "How did this happen? How did life turn around for you?" His answer is going to have "Jesus" somewhere in the first sentence. The name of his company is Champion. His logo is David's five smooth stones. I have watched Jesus conquer giant after giant in this man's life, so the brand is fitting. There are still other giants, but now he knows how to use the weapons.

Now, obviously, my friend never suffered from leprosy. So why did I tell his story here? Because when we live in isolation from years of spiritual and emotional numbness brought on by personal failure and shame, doesn't it produce a similar outcome in this culture? I have certainly felt the personal effects of this emotional version of the disease myself.

Here's the story of a real leper turned leader in Scripture.

*Now on his way to Jerusalem, Jesus traveled along the border between Samaria and Galilee. As he was going into a village, ten men who had leprosy met him. They stood at a distance and called out in a loud voice, "Jesus, Master, have pity on us!" When he saw them, he said, "Go, show yourselves to the priests." And as they went, they were cleansed. One of them, when he saw he was healed, came back, praising God in a loud voice. He threw himself at Jesus' feet and thanked him. —Luke 17:11–15 NIV*

"So, Robert, how do you know this guy became a leader?" … Because the moment he realized he was healed, he quit following the crowd and went to worship the Lord. That's a sure sign of a leader changed by God.

Blues guitarist and singer Jonny Lang began his career at 13. His debut CD *Lie to Me* went platinum when he was just 15. In the next few years he played with B.B. King and toured with Aerosmith and the Rolling Stones. Jonny shared, "By the time I was 17, I was an alcoholic and smoking two packs a day. I also started doing drugs. It was mostly marijuana, but I used cocaine, ecstasy, and hallucinogens. I really loved to be high. It got to be such a problem, that if I wasn't high I didn't feel normal.

I never really had an interest in religion. I saw things that really burned me and turned me off to Christianity—especially hypocrisy. However, what turned me off the most about Christianity was that I'd never seen the power of God move. It was just a lot of going through the motions, but not experiencing His power or His presence. And I certainly wasn't interested in being held accountable for my actions, which is basically what it all boils down to.

If anybody tried to talk to me about God or Jesus I would say things like, 'Okay, I've heard that one and I'm not interested.' I got involved in a lot of less accepted forms of spiritual expression that I thought were the right path, but I found out later where the real power is."

In the year 2000, Jonny met Jesus Christ in the backyard of his girlfriend's house, just after her father had died.

"The most convincing reason that I know He's real is that I know the person I was before I met Him. I know the way I thought and the way I conducted my life. That old person was replaced with a brand new one, a person who was willing to conform to the image of Christ. All the sermons in the world could not have convinced me of that. But He convinced me of Himself and I know the truth. I've witnessed so many wonders and miracles and God just proves himself to me constantly. There's nothing that could convince me otherwise. Jesus is the living God."[2]

Here's a verse from Jonny's testimony song, *Only a Man*.

*I grew up singing songs in church*
*With questions in my mind*
*Then turned my back and ran away*
*From God who gave me life*
*Then one night his presence fell*
*I wept and shook and then*
*I fell down and cried, Dear Jesus, rescue me again*
*I understand I am only a man*[3]

You just can't argue with a changed life, can you?

## DISCUSSION QUESTIONS

1.  Discuss these thoughts from Page 195: "Today, what causes two guys to accept Christ at the same time and one becomes a leader, while the other stays status quo? Two men join a Bible study group and one eventually drops out and disappears, while another can't seem to get enough of God. "

2.  Talk about this statement from Page 200: "Regardless of who you are, your background or belief, we are all serving and worshipping something. It's just a matter of what it is and whether it matters in the end or not." How do you see this be true in the lives of the men you know—Christian or not?

3.  Do you believe it is important for a man to decide who his "house will serve?" Why or why not?

4.  Discuss this statement from Page 201: "What you do for a paycheck, whether clerk, corporate, construction, or clergy doesn't matter as much as the purpose of your life being to serve Him and bring His will to Earth. What you do for a living just finances that ministry."

5.  Take the rest of the time allowing each man to briefly share his testimony. Share which one of the headings fits your story best and explain why: "Pagans to Priests," "Prodigals to Princes," "Lepers to Leaders."

## CHAPTER 15

# *FOLLOW THE KING*
# WE WILL SERVE THE LORD

*"Underneath this thing that I once was, now I'm a man of flesh and blood*
*I have a life beyond the grave, I found my heart, I can now be saved*
*No need to fear, I am not afraid, this Man of Sorrows took my pain*
*He comes to take away our sin and bear it's marks upon His skin*
*I'm telling you this story because, man of the tombs I was"* [1]
—*Bob Bennett*

I have always loved singer/songwriter Bob Bennett's musical take on the story of Legion's encounter with Jesus. It's one of those songs that I rarely hear without tears shed from sheer gratitude for my own salvation. Bob related his own story to Legion—and to Jesus' healing of him. I, too, relate my story through that incredible passage and the brilliance of this song. Using modern-day digital effects, this account would be an intense horror film. But as with so many Jesus stories, the horror ends when He enters the scene. Picture this as you read …

*They went across the lake to the region of the Gerasenes. When Jesus got out of the boat, a man with an evil spirit came from the tombs to meet him. This man lived in the tombs, and no one could bind him any more, not even with a chain. For he had often been chained hand and foot, but he tore the chains apart and broke the irons on his feet. No one was strong enough to subdue him. Night and day among the tombs and in the hills he would cry out and cut himself with stones.*

*When he saw Jesus from a distance, he ran and fell on his knees in front of him. He shouted at the top of his voice, "What do you want with me, Jesus, Son of the Most High God? Swear to God that you won't torture me!" For Jesus had said to him, "Come out of this man, you evil spirit!" Then Jesus asked him, "What is your name?" "My name is Legion," he replied, "for we are many." And he begged Jesus again and again not to send them out of the area.*

*A large herd of pigs was feeding on the nearby hillside. The demons begged Jesus, "Send us among the pigs; allow us to go into them." He gave them permission, and the evil spirits came out and went into the pigs. The herd, about two thousand in number, rushed down the steep bank into the lake and were drowned.*

*Those tending the pigs ran off and reported this in the town and countryside, and the people went out to see what had happened. When they came to Jesus, they saw the man who had been possessed by the legion of demons, sitting there, dressed and in his right mind; and they were afraid. Those who had seen it told the people what had happened to the demon-possessed man—and told about the pigs as well. Then the people began to plead with Jesus to leave their region.*

*As Jesus was getting into the boat, the man who had been demon-possessed begged to go with him. Jesus did not let him, but said, "Go home to your family and tell them how much the Lord has done for you, and how he has had mercy on you." So the man went away and began to tell in the Decapolis how much Jesus had done for him. And all the people were amazed.* —*Mark 5:1–20 NIV*

The details of this story are mind-boggling. This guy had a lot of demons in him, but one was in charge and spoke on behalf of the others—the creatures that caused this man to have super-human strength, made him self-destructive, (note the cutting), and caused him to make his home among the dead. A vital detail to pay attention to here is that when they just saw Jesus coming, they ALL submitted to Him. It's interesting how often when Jesus encountered demons, they always knew His presence signaled the end of their domination over whomever they were menacing. Their immediate submission to Christ is such great news for each of us and our personal issues. It teaches us that the key component to our own healing, to placing us in our "right mind," is submission to Christ. Hitting our knees in His presence as Legion did.

This delivered man's life is just as ours. The only difference is the amount of devastation the enemy levels on each life. But in this case, the pain of the past no longer mattered, because Jesus had assured his future. And that miracle should never stop amazing us.

When people heard what happened, and then saw this man whole, they asked Jesus to leave. Radical change just freaks a lot of people out. Unexplainable transformation rattles some folks, even religious ones. So the now peace-filled man obeyed Jesus and went home, testifying of what Christ had done and the people there were amazed. When we change and make sweeping 180's in our lives, some people will have nothing to do with us anymore, while others will be totally jazzed about it. And you just might be surprised into which group some people will fall.

## THE KING IS WORTHY TO FOLLOW BECAUSE HE CHANGES ... TRAITORS INTO TRANSLATORS

I've been a major *24* fan since I stumbled onto the TV series during one crazed September evening of channel surfing. It was around the third episode of season two, I believe. As with so many folks, one time and I was hooked. A major reason I became a Jack Bauer fan is because Jack will put all personal feelings aside and do the right thing, regardless of who agrees with him or if anyone else will come along and help. He'll go against the grain in a heartbeat to insure justice will prevail. Patriotism goes to a whole 'nother level with Mr. Bauer. Over eight seasons and 192 episodes, thousands upon thousands of American men found a hero in Jack Bauer.[2] Why? You can count on Jack.

Jack will get it done. Jack will go to any length, including personal sacrifice, to save the day. That's why.

One of the great aspects of *24* plots is there was always an unmistakeable line drawn between the good guys and the bad guys. Over here, you got your All-American counter-terrorist agents. Over there, you got your terrorists. Clear distinction. But there was always a third group you could count on too, even though it took a while to figure out who they were. … the traitors. Those who appeared to be good guys, but were really just bad guys in disguise. Of course, eventually, the truth would leak out, the stuff would hit the fan, and Jack would be after the bad guys *and* the traitors. Jack never liked bad guys, but he always held a special place in his heart for traitors. To Jack, at least the bad guys had the guts to be bad guys out in the open. Traitors were just above worm scum to Jack and he eventually let them know his deepest feelings about them—generally by some weapon or method of torture. The bottom line is you always knew what Jack would do with a traitor.

But what does God do with traitors? First, let's make the definition clear. A traitor is a turncoat, a defector, a deserter, one who betrays their original loyalties.

I've got good news, but first, some bad news. I'm a traitor. Yeah. I sit and eat with Jesus, then hours later kiss Him on the cheek and turn away to join the enemy. The Judas experience repeated over and over. How many times have I declared my allegiance to Christ with my hand held in the air in praise, my eyes filled with tears of gratitude, my lips declaring his goodness, and my heart filled with love, only to find within hours, I am selling Him out, turning my back, choosing my way, and acting as if I don't know Him? Can you relate to that? Isn't that the reality for us all when we choose to sin? Yeah, by definition of traitor, I often betray my God. So do you.

British Puritan theologian John Owen (1616–1683) wrote in his book, *Overcoming Sin and Temptation*, "We have no strength, no power to withstand, ... and, which is worse, it is the worst kind of weakness that is in us—a weakness from treachery. ... There are traitors in our hearts, ready to take part, to close and side with every temptation, and to give up all to them. ... there are secret lusts that lie lurking in your hearts, which perhaps now stir not, which, as soon as any temptation befalls you, will rise, cry, disquiet, seduce, and never give over until they are either killed or satisfied."[3] ... Sadly, this is all too true for the human condition.

But what does God do with traitors? What does He do with me? With you?

Let's go back to Jack for a moment. What if he captures the traitor and let's just say that he/she turns out to be a Russian agent? Jack looks the person in the eyes and in that menacing voice grits out, "Look, I'm not going to kill you. I'm not going to hurt you. I want you to help me translate the message of the hope and freedom of America to your fellow Russians."... What?!?!

God does just such a strange and paradoxical thing with traitors ... me ... you.

*All this is from God, who reconciled us to himself through Christ and gave us the ministry of reconciliation: that God was reconciling the world to himself in Christ, not counting men's sins against them. And he has committed to us the message of reconciliation. We are therefore Christ's ambassadors, as though God were making his appeal through us. We implore you on Christ's behalf: Be reconciled to God. God made him who had no sin to be sin for us, so that in him we might become the righteousness of God. —2 Corinthians 5:18–20 NIV*

God takes a man that He knows can betray Him at the very next turn and tells Him to be a translator in his culture, in His name. Why would He do this? Isn't there a better plan? ... No. Because God knows if a traitor keeps receiving

> GOD TAKES A MAN THAT HE KNOWS CAN BETRAY HIM AT THE VERY NEXT TURN AND TELLS HIM TO BE A TRANSLATOR IN HIS CULTURE, IN HIS NAME.

forgiveness and understanding that, over time, the joy of watching Him change lives through the translation of His life will overcome the desire to betray. Yes, it is slow, often very slow for some of us, but it does work. The big church word for this process is "sanctification."

Think about it. How long have you been a Christian? Whether your answer is three months or thirty years, isn't one of the very things that makes us love Him more as time passes, His great grace and continued desire to use us in His work? In spite of ourselves? The fact that He wants to involve us in the miracle of changing lives begins to slowly overcome our desire to hurt Him, to betray Him. In fact, it eventually really begins to sting us when we sting Him. We begin to see that translating the love of our God to our culture is far more satisfying and gratifying than trying to do life on our own, away from Him, betraying Him.

Paul was a traitor …

*Meanwhile, Saul was still breathing out murderous threats against the Lord's disciples. He went to the high priest and asked him for letters to the synagogues in Damascus, so that if he found any there who belonged to the Way, whether men or women, he might take them as prisoners to Jerusalem. —Acts 9:1–2 NIV*

… who became a translator.

*But whatever was to my profit I now consider loss for the sake of Christ. What is more, I consider everything a loss compared to the surpassing greatness of knowing Christ Jesus my Lord, for whose sake I have lost all things. I consider them rubbish, that I may gain Christ and be found in him, not having a righteousness of my own that comes from the law, but that which is through faith in Christ—the righteousness that comes from God and is by faith. I want to know Christ and the power of his resurrection and the fellowship of sharing in his sufferings, becoming like him in his death. —Philippians 3:7–10 NIV*

Are you serious? Really?! Is this the same guy? … Yep.

Paul went from being written about to writing about. Translating. Making a heavenly language understandable on Earth. God wants you to join Him in this same task, reaching the world for Him, with Him, by Him. What greater purpose could your life serve than following Him and watching Him translate His love through you to others? Changing the world one heart at a time. Turning other traitors into translators. Just like me. Just like you.

## THE KING IS WORTHY TO FOLLOW BECAUSE HE CHANGES ... FUGITIVES INTO FRIENDS

The world is full of fugitives. It has been ever since the Garden episode. What did Adam and Eve do after they sinned? They ran and hid from God. Just like a fugitive. Commit the crime. Realize guilt. Try to avoid consequences. Run!

Do you remember playing wiffleball and someone would hit a neighbor's car or break a window? What do all little boys do? Run! Why? Because something bad happened and you don't want to just stand there and take the blame, so you run and hide. You may have been picking your nose at shortstop, thinking about supper, but when everyone else ran, so did you.

But as we get older, we're cooler about our sin, aren't we? … Or are we? We tend to make sure things that we don't feel so good about happen at night, or at least in the dark. Nightclubs aren't pumpin' the jam and the booze at 1 p.m. Prostitutes don't fill the street corner at 10 a.m. Men don't meet their mistresses out in front of their house. Thieves typically lie in wait until nightfall to break in. Why? We know to do our bad things in the dark, away from the light, out of plain sight.

*What shall we conclude then? Are we any better? Not at all! We have already made the charge that Jews and Gentiles alike are all under sin. As it is written: "There is no one righteous, not even one; there is no one who understands, no one who seeks God. All have turned away, they have*

*together become worthless; there is no one who does good, not even one.*
—*Romans 3:9–12* NIV

… We're all fugitives.

In the classic movie with Harrison Ford and Tommy Lee Jones, *The Fugitive*, there is a climactic scene where Dr. Richard Kimble (Ford) is trying to escape—again—from Chief Deputy Marshal Gerard (Jones) down in the laundry room of the hotel after he's confronted Dr. Nichols, who we now know is behind the murder and cover-up. Gerard calls out, "Kimble! I know you didn't kill your wife!"[4]… We all let out a huge sigh of relief at that moment. And so did Dr. Kimble. Why? Because we all knew the nearly two hours of running and narrow escapes could stop. Finally—relief from running. No more hiding.

How many of us guys just can't seem to stop running? Running from our past. Running from failures. Running from responsibility. Running from facing ourselves. And too often, running from whom we know God desires us to be.

Why do we run? What are we afraid will happen if we stop? Do we not think that God can catch us if He wants? Here's a verse to settle us down and make us think.

*I no longer call you servants, because a servant does not know his master's business. Instead, I have called you friends, for everything that I learned from my Father I have made known to you.* —*John 15:15* NIV

This is a bit logical, I know, but you cannot make friends with someone you are running away from, can you? The sooner we figure out that He is standing in the same place where He has always been standing, then we know exactly where to go to meet our Friend.

But we are running in the same way Adam and Eve ran in the Garden, for the same reasons. So God calls out to me, "Robert! I gave the life of My Son, so you can stop running!" He calls out to you by name as well.

God wants the death and resurrection of Jesus to end the hiding, for you to accept that He has paid your ransom, and offered you redemption and freedom. Today, He desires to be your Friend. Today, you can be His friend. He wants you in on His business in His inner circle. So we must …

*"Seek first his kingdom and his righteousness, and all these things will be given to you as well." —Matthew 6:33 NIV*

My personal translation of this verse is: "When you take care of the mission that I give you in the way I want it done, I will take care of all your life." What has to happen before "all these things are given?" We must "seek" Him.

Fugitives don't seek, they run. Friends don't run, they seek.

## THE THREE S'S

We can be changed from a pagan to a priest, from a prodigal to a prince, from a leper to a leader, from a traitor to a translator, and from a fugitive to a friend when we agree to:

Surrender ➜ Submit ➜ Serve

Surrender means to give up the fight, give over control, abandon your rights, and declare defeat.

Submit means to yield to, agree to, or defer to.

The Biblical process of surrender and submission is giving up your life and taking on His. Again, crawling up on the altar (Romans 12:1–2).

After this process has begun, the assignment is to serve. But here's the cool thing that took me a very long time to understand—and I'm still working on daily. God does not bark out orders, telling you to get out of His face and get to work. He walks with you, as a Friend, and you work together as a team. He does this with all His followers. How can He possibly do this? Because He is God. He is King.

*However, I consider my life worth nothing to me, if only I may finish the race and complete the task the Lord Jesus has given me—the task of testifying to the gospel of God's grace. —Acts 20:24 NIV*

Paul's declaration of testifying to God's grace was a lifestyle, not an event. It was an every-day, as-you-go, way of life. As I live, I represent God. As I go, I translate His Word and His love to those I come in contact with. So how do you know what to do? He tells you. Listen for His voice. Obey what you hear.

As you go, as you live your life, remember the Three Ss—Surrender, Submit, and Serve. In that order. So, what do you do if you mess up today and disobey God? Ask His forgiveness. Surrender, Submit, and then start serving again. No wallowing. No emotional beat-downs. No wasting precious time. Get right back to the Three S's ASAP.

## Surveying the Battlefield

In closing, I want to give you a scenario, an inspiration, and some practical help to press on from here.

If you and I were placed in a situation where our families were threatened—their safety and their very lives put on the line. And we can't call 9-1-1. We can't call the police, the Armed Forces, or any outside help. Our only chance is for you and I to rally together to fight the enemy coming to destroy our families and our homes. I don't know about you, but I would want some weapons. In fact, I would prefer an arsenal to call upon. I suppose with enough anger and adrenaline, bare hands might cause some damage, but to hold out and take the enemy completely out, we're going to need some real leverage. Let's inventory what we got. I got a pistol and a shotgun. Great. You got a deer rifle and a Rambo knife. Perfect. Now, let's get all the bullets and shells out and ready. Okay, we're starting to think we might could pull this off.

Well, gentlemen, in this life, in this world, that really is where we are. There is a definite spiritual battle going on to end our marriages, destroy our children, and take us out. We have an enemy who wants to rob, kill, and destroy (John 10:10) and he'll take any or all of those three he can get. Take everything away from you and go in for the kill. Pick us off one by one. Stop our effectiveness in order to hurt God.

Whether you are a Christian or not, a spiritual man or not, you are affected by this battle. You are in it—believe it or not, like it or not. Denying it doesn't make it untrue. You are either fighting the battle or being fought, or maybe you're just a pawn in the enemy's hands, being used to hurt others. Regardless, the war between God and Satan, the angels and demons, the heavenly army and the underworld is going down right now—everywhere. Just look around. How far do you have to go in your world to find a family that's crumbling? When was the last time you got bad news about a friend's downfall? Read or watched the news lately? See how well everything is going? The battle is real and you know it.

> WHETHER YOU ARE A CHRISTIAN OR NOT, A SPIRITUAL MAN OR NOT, YOU ARE AFFECTED BY THIS BATTLE. YOU ARE IN IT—BELIEVE IT OR NOT, LIKE IT OR NOT.

I hope you have decided to be certain you are on God's side. To accept His offer to adopt you as His son. To join His army as a warrior for Him. Like the knights of medieval days committed to their king, to ride under the banner of Christ. To battle the god of this world. Your allegiance given to the King of kings.

But in this supernatural battle, we need some very specialized weapons to fight. Rifles, pistols, even swords, don't work in this war. It's a battle of the heart, of the soul. I want to show you an arsenal that you can put into place in your life today—to help you live out purity, truth, and justice on a daily basis. Here we go …

**Tenet 1: Live Pure**
**Goal: Empowered by God's purity**
**Weapon: God's Word**
**Tactical Use: Reading, studying, and memorizing the Holy Scripture**

*God means what he says. What he says goes. His powerful Word is sharp as a surgeon's scalpel, cutting through everything, whether doubt or defense, laying us open to listen and obey. Nothing and no one is impervious to God's Word. We can't get away from it—no matter what.*

*—Hebrews 4:12* MSG

*Blessed is the man who does not walk in the counsel of the wicked or stand in the way of sinners or sit in the seat of mockers. But his delight is in the law of the* LORD, *and on his law he meditates day and night.*

*—Psalm 1:1–2* NIV

*I gain understanding from your precepts; therefore I hate every wrong path. Your word is a lamp to my feet and a light for my path. I have taken an oath and confirmed it, that I will follow your righteous laws.*

*—Psalm 119:104–106* NIV

Consistent reading, studying, and memorization of God's Word is the only eternal replacement in our souls for the sin, evil, junk, and garbage we take in and the world throws at us. A very miraculous, amazing thing that God does when we ingest His Word is to bring up the appropriate Scripture to our minds and out of our mouths at exactly the point we need it to minister to our own hearts or others, both to protect us and advance the Kingdom.

I have had countless situations over thirty years where a Scripture came from my mouth that I had not intentionally memorized, but I had read it enough that it was placed in my spirit, and when needed, the Holy Spirit brought it out to be used in the battle. This is a major weapon that God will be certain we wield in a surprising fashion at the right time. His Word used by His Spirit.

And, obviously, Scripture that we intentionally memorize can be used easily and often, but God will always multiply your time in His Word. Scripture will protect you, your family, and your circles of influence. If you're already in His Word, keep going deeper. If you're not, begin today. The enemy does not want you to take in Scripture, because it is one of our strongest weapons against him and to protect us, as seen when Jesus used it in His temptations (Matthew 4:1–11).

Tenet 2: Speak True
Goal: Transformed by God's truth
Weapon: Accountability
Tactical Use: Sharing life with brothers for the purpose of spiritual growth and moral protection

*If one falls down, his friend can help him up. But pity the man who falls and has no one to help him up! … Though one may be overpowered, two can defend themselves. A cord of three strands is not quickly broken.*
                                        —*Ecclesiastes 4:10, 12 NIV*

*As iron sharpens iron, so one man sharpens another.*
                                        —*Proverbs 27:17 NIV*

*Therefore confess your sins to each other and pray for each other so that you may be healed. The prayer of a righteous man is powerful and effective. … My brothers, if one of you should wander from the truth and someone should bring him back, remember this: Whoever turns a sinner from the error of his way will save him from death and cover over a multitude of sins.* —*James 5:16, 19–20 NIV*

*Be very careful, then, how you live—not as unwise but as wise, making the most of every opportunity, because the days are evil. Therefore do not be foolish, but understand what the Lord's will is. … Submit to one another out of reverence for Christ.* —*Ephesians 5:15–16, 21 NIV*

*Live creatively, friends. If someone falls into sin, forgivingly restore him, saving your critical comments for yourself. You might be needing forgiveness before the day's out. Stoop down and reach out to those who are oppressed. Share their burdens, and so complete Christ's law. If you think you are too good for that, you are badly deceived.* —*Galatians 6:1–3 MSG*

We have talked plenty about this topic in other places in the book, so I will be brief here.

Nothing will keep us on track with truth quite like the encouragement and protection of other brothers. A like-minded and like-hearted circle of men that can have your back and kick your butt. The right group of brothers in our lives can slowly help us move the lies out and usher the truth in. Bottom line is it's just harder to fake life and smile pretty when we have to tell someone the real truth on a regular basis.

When accountability or protection is done right, it turns from "have to" to "get to." *"I have to go to this group meeting tonight. Man, it's hard having to answer those questions every week."* Over time and some victories, that can transition to, *"I am so grateful I get to go to my group. Those guys saved my life last week."*

As men we tend to judge ourselves too harshly on some issues, while we let ourselves off the hook too easily on others. We can make some areas of life way too hard, while we get lazy in other places. A band of brothers can balance that out. A band of brothers can save each other's lives, marriages, kids, jobs, and an assortment of other strategic areas.

What can keep your car from breaking down at crucial times? What can keep you off the side of the highway in a life-threatening situation? Regular vehicle maintenance, right? Your group meeting is about heart and soul maintenance. Maintenance that can help keep you out of crises and a moral break-down.

I call this a *Three Strand Group* or *3SG* from *"a cord of three strands is not quickly broken"* in Ecclesiastes 4:10–12. Whatever you choose to call it—a growth group, small group, protection group, or account-ability meeting, it's like the power of the wind. You may not can see it, but you will definitely feel the results when it's strong.

**Tenet 3: Right Wrong**
**Goal: Joining God's justice**
**Weapon: Principles**
**Tactical Use: Setting life boundaries for the purpose of spiritual growth and moral protection**

We have touched on principles in a number of sections through-out this book, but we discussed principles of protection in detail in Chapter 9.

Quick recap: A principle is a guide or rule that you set for yourself. The idea is that you create offensive and defensive principles to maintain God's justice in your life. Justice in this setting refers to maintaining personal righteousness, fairness, and balance by a system of Biblical reasoning. In short, setting public boundaries to maintain private balance.

An offensive principle is a pro-active approach to growing spiritually. A defensive principle is to keep from committing a wrong that will have to be made right. In short, you keep the rights right and the wrongs to a minimum. But when you do wrong (as we all will), you right it as quickly as possible, using God's ways. ... Capeche?

**Tenet 4: Follow the King**
**Goal: Practicing God's presence**
**Weapon: Time**
**Tactical Use: Investing the intentional moments to speak with, listen to, and rest in the presence of Christ**

*Very early in the morning, while it was still dark, Jesus got up, left the house and went off to a solitary place, where he prayed. —Mark 1:35 NIV*

This verse is why I call spending dedicated time with God a *One-Thirty-Five Time* or a *One35*. Let's take this verse apart and look deep into the hidden mysteries of the Greek language to pull out what this verse is really saying. Ready?

1. He got up early.

2. He went off by Himself.

3. He prayed.

Pretty amazing what you can get when you study the original languages, huh? Okay, for you extra dry guys, I am kidding about the languages thing. This verse says what it means, it means what it says.

It's also a safe bet, and probably not taking liberty with the Scripture, to say that Jesus didn't have *CNN* or *Sports Center* on. He got away from everyone and ALL distractions and focused on ONE thing—His

Heavenly Father. He prayed. He listened. He received what He needed to be able to handle His day. (The reason for the enhanced One in *One35*—the One thing we focus on during that time is Christ.)

Talking to your Heavenly Dad about life and then listening to Him, reading His Word, that's nothing but a solid move to live life right. After all, it's what He did. So who are we to think we don't need it? I don't just need it, I have to have it to survive and then to thrive.

Whatever block of time you set aside to pray, the idea is not that, after a few minutes alone with Him, you tell Jesus goodbye until tomorrow morning when you show up again. Your *One35 Time* kicks off the conversation between you and Him that will take place all day long. You can pray silently, or just talk to Him out loud whenever possible. In today's Bluetooth world, no one will notice anyway. Learning to speak to Him anytime, day or night, and listen for His voice is crucial to your victory in the battle. He has the right to interrupt your day and tell you anything He wants. Who's your Daddy? He is. Who's the King? He is!

Often when I teach on this topic, I use the following object lesson. I have a plastic chain with large links I bought at Lowe's. I intentionally counted out and bought a chain with 168 links. Why 168? That's the number of hours in a week. Seven days X 24 hours each. The particular chain I have is between seven and eight feet, so when I hold it up, 168 links looks like a lot. Then I ask the men this question, "What is a realistic amount of time a growing Christian should allow each day to spend time with God? I typically get answers from ten minutes to thirty minutes. Let's go for a really spiritual time with 30 minutes a day. 30 X 7 = 210 minutes or three-and-a-half hours. That is three-and-a-half links on my chain. Then I grab somewhere in the middle of the chain and, with both hands, hold up and mark off three-and-a-half links. It does not look like very much at all, with the rest of the chain hanging down almost to the floor on each side. And, in the span of 168 hours, I suppose it isn't much time. But most all guys would agree that a half hour a day would make a great prayer time and, over months, make for some strong spiritual growth. One of the interesting things about guys being both visual and competitive is that they look at those three-and-a-half links and think, "I can do more than that! That looks pitiful."

Here's the bottom line: we all know we will put the time and energy into the things that really matter to us. Author, professor, and communicator Tony Campolo often teaches, "The thing you think about the most is likely your god." The thing we think about the most is also what we will be placing time and energy into. That's what Tony means with his statement.

> WE ALL KNOW WE WILL PUT THE TIME AND ENERGY INTO THE THINGS THAT REALLY MATTER TO US.

God never called us to move into the mountains to become monks and devote every waking thought to Him. He did, however, call each of us into a relationship with Him where we go into the world, making disciples as we live our lives for Him. … Mind if I repeat that for emphasis? … Thanks. … God never called us to move into the mountains to become monks and devote every waking thought to Him. He did, however, call each of us into a relationship with Him where we go into the world, making disciples as we live our lives for Him. The time we spend talking and listening to Him is crucial for us to make disciples—of ourselves and others.

> *Then Jesus came to them and said, "All authority in heaven and on earth has been given to me. Therefore go and make disciples of all nations, baptizing them in the name of the Father and of the Son and of the Holy Spirit, and teaching them to obey everything I have commanded you. And surely I am with you always, to the very end of the age."*
>
> *—Matthew 28:18–20 NIV*

I love *The Message* version, same passage:

> *Jesus, undeterred, went right ahead and gave his charge: "God authorized and commanded me to commission you: Go out and train everyone you meet, far and near, in this way of life, marking them by baptism in*

*the threefold name: Father, Son, and Holy Spirit. Then instruct them in the practice of all I have commanded you. I'll be with you as you do this, day after day after day, right up to the end of the age."*

Sir, please don't miss this. Get this! The Living God has called your name and wants you to be His friend and confidant to change the world. What higher calling could you possibly be offered? What greater satisfaction in life could there possibly be? What greater love has any man than this? "A man has to have a code, a creed to live by, no matter his job."

Know this—God believes in you and is inviting you into His presence forever to live for Him as an heir and adopted son.

I want to challenge you to press on into the rest of your life with these four simple phrases in your heart—Live Pure, Speak True, Right Wrong, and Follow the King!

I leave you with Paul's challenge to us as Christ's warriors.

*And that about wraps it up. God is strong, and he wants you strong. So take everything the Master has set out for you, well-made weapons of the best materials. And put them to use so you will be able to stand up to everything the Devil throws your way. This is no afternoon athletic contest that we'll walk away from and forget about in a couple of hours. This is for keeps, a life-or-death fight to the finish against the Devil and all his angels.*

*Be prepared. You're up against far more than you can handle on your own. Take all the help you can get, every weapon God has issued, so that when it's all over but the shouting you'll still be on your feet. Truth, righteousness, peace, faith, and salvation are more than words. Learn how to apply them. You'll need them throughout your life. God's Word is an indispensable weapon. In the same way, prayer is essential in this ongoing warfare. Pray hard and long. Pray for your brothers and sisters. Keep your eyes open. Keep each other's spirits up so that no one falls behind or drops out. —Ephesians 6:10–18 MSG*

You ready? … Let's go …

## DISCUSSION QUESTIONS

1.  Discuss how our lives before Christ parallel to the story of Legion. Read Bob Bennett's lyrics on Page 213 to help the analogy.

2.  Why do you think God would allow us as traitors against Him to become translators for Him? Would you allow that? How can this concept work? (p. 215)

3.  Talk about running away from God versus running to God when you sin? How are you growing in that area? Talk about your progress.

4.  Regarding the Three S's on Page 221—Surrender, Submit, Serve—how can we practically work on shortening our "wallowing" and "emotional beat-down" time and move quicker into the process of the S's?

5.  Take the rest of the time and discuss the four Tenets and their Goals, Weapons, and Tactical Uses on Pages 223–229. Lay out a practical strategy to help each other grow in each of these areas. Answer questions such as: How often should you meet? How will you stay in touch between meetings for accountability? What does a man do, who does he call, if he gets into trouble?

## DISCUSSION QUESTIONS FOR FINAL GROUP MEETING

1. Through the entire book, discuss the one major life change point for you.

2. Share a breakthrough or victory you have had as a result of going through this book.

3. Share a struggle that this book helped bring to light and how you need help to fight moving forward.

   For helps on resources to continue your group, go to www.theknightscode.com.

## GETTING SERIOUS ABOUT A RELATIONSHIP WITH JESUS

There is a God-shaped void, or emptiness, inside every person. Each of us feels that void and attempts to fill it in our own way. We can put a lot of things into our heart, but they don't satisfy. Likely, His Holy Spirit is now helping you to see that He is the answer to that void in your life.

Jesus said in John 14:6, *"I am the way and the truth and the life. No one comes to the Father except through me."* Many religions or belief systems assume that humans have the power within themselves to correct their wrong attitudes and actions—that all they need to do is discover and develop that power. Christianity is based on the fact that we are born with the same nature as Adam and Eve, who decided to disobey God in the Garden of Eden (Genesis 3). We also have chosen to disobey him (Romans 7:15–20). We are guilty before a holy God, so we need His power (Romans 8:8).

Jesus—Who is God—experienced life as a human being (Hebrews 4:15). The wages—what we have earned—of our disobedience to God is death (Romans 6:23). The holiness of God demands punishment by death for this. Before Christ, the high priest sacrificed a lamb or bull in place of the person desiring forgiveness for sins. Jesus offered Himself as the final sacrifice (Hebrews 7:27). He died so that you wouldn't have to. Christ died in your place!

Christ—innocent of sin—took our punishment for us, giving His own life for each of us. John 15:13 says, *"Greater love has no one than this, that he lay down his life for his friends."* Each person must decide whether or not to accept Jesus' death as the replacement or substitution for his own. God, in His great love, gives you the choice!

Once you have agreed He is your Savior, (Romans 10:9–10) you are a new creation (2 Corinthians 5:17). You can live in His forgiveness (Galatians 2:20, Hebrews 8:12). You are saved by the grace of God (Ephesians 2:8–9), and freed, in His eyes, from past mistakes to live a life of serving Him and others in His power (Colossians 1:28–29).

If you are ready to begin a relationship with Him, simply accept His gift by praying a simple prayer like this:

*Dear God, I know I am a sinner and need Your forgiveness. I now turn from my sins and ask You into my life to be my Savior and Lord. Please forgive me. Thank You for dying for me, saving me, and giving me eternal life. In Jesus' name. Amen.*

If you prayed this prayer for the first time or you have before, but you sense a real difference this time, you need to let someone know. Contact a pastor or a trusted Christian friend and tell them about this prayer you prayed. Now, follow the King!

# NOTES

**Chapter 1**

1. StarWars.com, Lucas Online, Lucasfilm,Ltd., 2010, *Databank: Yoda,* http://www.starwars.com/databank/character/yoda/ (July 28, 2010)

**Chapter 2**

1. Pilar Wayne, *My Life With the Duke* (New York: McGraw-Hill Book Company, 1987), p. 7
2. Alfred Lord Tennyson, "Gareth and Lynette," in J. M. Gray, ed., *Idylls of the King* (New York: Penguin Classics, 1989), p. 39
3. Christopher Gravett, "The First Knights," *Knight* (New York: Alfred A. Knopf, Inc., 1993), pp. 6–7
4. Ibid., "The Ideal of Chivalry," pp. 40–41
5. Ibid.
6. Ibid., "Knights of Christ," pp. 56–57
7. Ibid., "The Decline of Chivalry," pp. 62–63
8. Legends of America, *Old West Legends: The Code of the West,* http://www.legendsofamerica.com/we-codewest.html (August 4, 2010)
9. Ralph Arnold, "The Rules of Chivalry," *Kings, Bishops, Knights, and Pawns* (New York: W. W. Norton & Company, 1963), p. 82
10. Gravett, op.cit., "Making a Knight," pp. 10–11
11. *A Knight's Tale,* http://www.imdb.com/title/tt0183790/ (August 4, 2010).
12. Arnold, op.cit., p. 81
13. Ibid.
14. *Kingdom of Heaven,* http://www.youtube.com/watch?v=10HnXc406lg&feature=related (July 28, 2010)
15. Arnold, op.cit., pp. 81–82
16. James Harper, "Medieval Knights," *Warriors: All the Truths, Tactics, and Triumphs of History's Greatest Fighters* (New York: Atheneum Books, 2007), pp. 22–23

**Chapter 3**

1. From the song, "Man in the Mirror" written by Glen Ballard and Seidah Garrett, recorded by Michael Jackson on the *Bad* project, 1987
2. The Edmund Burke Institute, http://edmundburkeinstitute.wordpress.com/ (August 4, 2010)
3. Harold "Hal" Moore, http://en.wikipedia.org/wiki/Hal_Moore,
4. *Hal Moore Played by Mel Gibson,* http://www.youtube.com/watch?v=w3c8Xr8NW4Y (August 4, 2010)
5. *The Guardian,* http://www.imdb.com/title/tt0406816/quotes (August 4, 2010)

## Chapter 4

1. From the song, "The Living Years" written by Mike Rutherford and B. A. Robertson, recorded by Mike & the Mechanics on the *The Living Years* project, 1989
2. Kenny Rogers' *The Gambler,* http://www.answers.com/topic/the-gambler-song (August 4, 2010)
3. *A Knight's Tale,* http://www.imdb.com/title/tt0183790/quotes (August 4, 2010)

## Chapter 5

1. From the song, "Matters of the Heart" written by Michael McDonald, recorded by Michael McDonald on the *Blink of an Eye* project, p. 199
2. Ted Steinberg, "Live Free and Mow," *American Green: The Obsessive Quest for the Perfect Lawn* (New York: W.W. Norton & Company, 2006), p. 5

## Chapter 6

1. From the song, "The Way It Is" written by Bruce Hornsby, recorded by Bruce Hornsby & the Range on the *The Way It Is* project, 1986

## Chapter 7

1. From the song, "Dragons" written by Edwin McCain, recorded by Edwin McCain on the *Far from Over* project, 2001

## Chapter 8

1. From the song, "Imaginary Lover" written by Buie/Nix/Daughtry/Bailey, recorded by Atlanta Rhythm Section on the *Champagne Jam* project, 1978
2. "Rattlesnake Kiss Lands Man in Hospital," Fort Worth Star Telegram, November 19, 2002
3. "Women addicted to porn: sites are no longer attracting just men," AG.org News & Information, March 22, 2010 (http://rss. ag.org/articles/detail.cfm?RSS_RSSContentID=14913&RSS_OriginatingChannelID=1007&RSS_OriginatingRSSFeedID=1034&RSS_Source=websiteGUID_35cfdda9-0172-4bc3-898d-14caf7003e2a) (August 4, 2010)

## Chapter 9

1. From the song, "Lord, Save Me from Myself" written by Jon Foreman, recorded by Jon Foreman on the *Fall* project, 2007
2. Alcoholics Anonymous, *A Brief Guide to Alcoholics Anonymous,* (New York, 1972), p. 13
3. Ibid., p. 14
4. Evangelism Today, *Leaders Insight: When Leaders Implode,* http://evangelismtoday.blogspot.com/2006/11/leaders-insight-when-leaders-implode.html#_ednref2 (August 5, 2010)
5. Steve Farrar, *Finishing Strong,* (Oregon: Multnomah Books, 1995), pp. 5–6

**Chapter 10**
1. From the song, "My Stupid Mouth" written by John Mayer, recorded by John Mayer on the *Room for Squares* project, 2001
2. Georges Duby, *William Marshall: The Flower of Chivalry* (New York: Pantheon Books, 1985), p. 25
3. Catherine Armstrong, *William Marshall, Earl of Pembroke,* http://www.castlewales.com/marshall.html (1998)

**Chapter 11**
1. From the song, "The Heart of the Matter" written by Campbell/Henley/Souther, recorded by Don Henley on the *The End of the Innocence* project, 1989
2. Chris Carrier, *I Faced My Killer Again,* Christianity Today International, April 22, 1997, http://www.christianity.com/Christian%20Living/Features/11622274/ (August 5, 2010)

**Chapter 12**
1. From the song, "Hole in My Life" written by Sting, recorded by Sting on the *iTunes Originals* project, 2004
2. Kathy Gill, *The Military Draft,* About.com: U.S. Politics http://uspolitics.about.com/od/thedraft/i/the_draft.htm (August 5, 2010)
3. U.S. Marines, *Semper Fidelis: More Than a Motto, A Way of Life,* http://www.marines.com/main/index/making_marines/culture/traditions/semper_fidelis (August 5, 2010)
4. Marilyn White, I Go Pogo, *"We have met the enemy … and he is us,"* http://www.igopogo.com/we_have_met.htm (August 5, 2010)
5. Sandra Sobieraj Westfall, "Elin Nordegren My Journey," *People,* September 6, 2010, Vol. 74, No. 7
6. Courtney Hazlett, "The Scoop," *Today Show,* December 2, 2009 (http://today.msnbc.msn.com/id/34243626) (September 1, 2010)
7. Sandra Sobieraj Westfall, "Elin Nordegren My Journey," *People,* September 6, 2010, Vol. 74, No. 7
8. Brian Regan, *Dinner Party,* I Walked on the Moon DVD

**Chapter 13**
1. From the song, "All Fall Down" written by Brown/Filkins/Fisher/Kutzle/Tedder, recorded by OneRepublic on the *Dreaming Out Loud* project, 2007
2. *Robin Hood: Prince of Thieves,* http://www.imdb.com/title/tt0102798/quotes (August 9, 2010)

## Chapter 14

1. From the song, "Walls" written by Bryce Avary, recorded by The Rocket Summer on the *Of Men and Angels* project, 2010
2. Amy Hammond Hagberg, *Jonny Lang's Testimony*, How Do You Know He's Real: God Unplugged, October 24, 2006 (http://www.cmspin.com/newsmanager/anmviewer.asp?a=3951&z=51) (August 10, 2010)
3. From the song, "Only a Man" written by Jonny Lang, recorded by Jonny Lang on the *Turn Around* project, 2006

## Chapter 15

1. From the song, "Man of the Tombs" written by Bob Bennett, recorded by Bob Bennett on the *The View From Here* project, 2001
2. George Fergus, 24—*A Titles & Air Dates Guide,* epguides.com, http://epguides.com/24/ (August 10, 2010)
3. *Overcoming Sin and Temptation* by John Owen, Edited by Kelly M. Kapic and Justin Taylor, Crossway Books, September 25, 2006, p. 171
4. *The Fugitive,* http://www.imdb.com/title/tt0106977/(August 10, 2010)

For more
information
and
resources,

visit
WWW.THEKNIGHTSCODE.COM